A Poke
in the Public Eye

Media Manipulation for Aspiring
Politicians and Other Undesirables

David J. Climenhaga

Detselig Enterprises Ltd.
Calgary, Alberta, Canada

A Poke in the Public Eye

© 1995 David Climenhaga

Canadian Cataloguing in Publication Data

Climenhaga, David J., 1952-
  A poke in the public eye

ISBN 1-55059-110-X

  Mass media--Political aspects--Humor. 2 Public relations
and politics--Humor. 3. Politicians--Humor. I. Title.
P91.C64 1995   302.23'088327   C95-910582-4

Detselig Enterprises Ltd.
210, 1220 Kensington Rd. NW
Calgary, AB T2N 3P5

Cover Design by Dean MacDonald

Printed in Canada   SAN 115-0324   ISBN 1-55059-110-X

To Katie and Lily

Acknowledgments

As I note later in the pages of this tome, I have the good fortune to work in a place where my colleagues make lies out of my complaints about the organized practice of journalism. I owe my good work mates, who daily commit journalism that serves the public honorably and well, a debt of gratitude for the seriousness with which they practice (and constantly talk about) their craft and their fine, dark humor (which I have mostly failed to acknowledge where used). I pray they will forgive me for the bad jokes cracked herein seemingly at their expense. They were not the ones I had in mind.

Likewise, let me both thank and say sorry to the many decent politicians I have known, who serve the public well in lowly office for a pittance. If some of you phoned me at home on my time off to trumpet some dubious achievement, you're forgiven. If some of you had to put up with me phoning you to complain about airplane flights over my house or dogs in the park, well that − like gratuitous insults − goes with the territory, doesn't it?

Thanks also to my friends in journalism, John Thomson and Margaret MacNabb, who read parts of my manuscript and suggested worthwhile changes. And to Tara Gregg of Detselig Enterprises Ltd., whose editing was easy to live with. (All the mistakes, as they say, are entirely . . . mine.) And to Dave Olecko, who took my picture and managed to make me look relatively thin. And to the late Doug MacRae who, for good or ill, got me my first real job in the news business nearly a quarter of a century ago by telling an editor "the kid can spell cat." (Eventually, thanks in no small part to Doug, I could.)

Above all, I must thank my wife Luanne and my beautiful girls Kate and Lily, who must have wondered what the heck I was doing typing and typing into the wee hours of the morning. Come to think of it, they must be wondering that right now.

Thanks!

Detselig Enterprises Ltd. appreciates the financial support for our 1995 publishing program, provided by the Department of Canadian Heritage, Canada Council and the Alberta Foundation for the Arts, a beneficiary of the Lottery Fund of the Government of Alberta.

Contents

Introduction   7

Basic Media Manipulation

1 — Getting Ready to Manipulate   13
2 — Understanding the Media   23
3 — Dressing for Political Success   37

Intermediate Media Manipulation

4 — How to Write Effective News Releases   47
5 — Feeding and Watering the Media   63

Advanced Media Manipulation

6 — Leaking Confidentially   71
7 — Friendships and Favoritism   81
8 — Holy Writs and Damning Prose   93
9 — Dave's Handy Checklist   105

Graduate Studies

Appendix I – An Actual Effective News Release   117
Appendix II – An Actual Ineffective News Release   119
Glossary   125

Warning

This is not exactly a work of fiction, but the author could not resist using some of the techniques of the genre. So, while the general circumstances and complaints described are real enough, the characters described – where not clearly identified by the names of actual public figures – are not. Any similarity between them and real people living or dead are, as they say, entirely coincidental.

Introduction

Every year in Canada, literally thousands of citizens, quite a few of them functionally unemployed, make a bid to get themselves elected to public office. Virtually none of them has a clue, let alone a hope.

This urge becomes most pressing just after, or just before, a well-publicized federal or provincial election. For example, in a by-election in Calgary in 1993 – as it happened, the year of both a provincial and federal election – no fewer than 23 fevered individuals signed up on nomination day to run for alderman in a single city ward. By custom, the winner had to live there. And it wasn't even a particularly nice part of town! Hardly anyone outside their immediate families had heard of any of them. Most ran because they needed a job. A couple because they needed a hobby, or even (the reporter covering the election* suspected) a hubby.

Yet, even if on some atavistic level such people recognize that they've got about as much chance of getting elected as a dyslexic has of being chosen as president of the proofreaders' society, Canadians nevertheless line up to run for alderman, school trustee and community association social convener. If dog catchers had to be elected in Canada, they'd be queuing up for that too.

Most of these lost souls are, of course, doomed come election day, as are their $100 deposits.

The fact is, the vast majority of these wretched seekers after insignificant civic political office are naive, deluded, even outright stupid. Indeed, there is an argument in journalistic and some political circles that, come nomination day, someone ought to just back a yellow school bus up to the loading dock at city hall, ask anyone who's actually signed nomination papers and

---

* Yours Truly

put down their deposit to step aboard, then drive 'em off for a 30-day psychiatric remand.

Still, while most of these candidates for petty political office screw up because they're too dumb, too lost, too confused, or just too darn weird, some reasonably bright and articulate hopefuls mess up too. More often than not, it's because of some dreadful and needless miscalculation in their relations with the news media.

When they do, the pathetic loser who flukes into office in their stead will often soon make a similarly gross miscalculation in media relations and pay by losing a perfectly good publicly financed job after only three or four years. (For example, it's all very well to force the fire chief to drive you home after the mayor's annual Halloween booze-up. All reasonable voters understand that they'd do exactly the same thing if they were wearing your gumboots, so they'll find it easy to forgive you. Just don't issue a press release bragging about what a good example you're setting by not driving drunk through crowds of costumed munchkins in the huge new Chrysler New Yorker you just bought with your aldermanic car allowance. That would be stupid. Leave out the part about the New Yorker!)

Yet many of these same aspiring politicians are bound to ask: "Should I bother even trying to manipulate the media?"

Presumably they ask this question because they are clueless. Either that, or they've just returned from three decades on an Anabaptist commune in Brazil. It is an extremely foolish question. The answer is obvious: You die without manipulating the media. Free publicity is the oxygen of politics. And the media is the only show in town when it comes to getting it. You don't seriously think that these guys are going to come to you just because you have something worthwhile to say, do you?

If you're one of the multitude of office-seekers and you can't figure out this elementary fact, don't give up your day job. That's probably sound advice anyway. Because, yes, while there are good reasons for running for public office in Canada during the late 20th century – mainly the pension benefits – there are also plenty of better-looking, smarter, richer people with precisely the same ambition as you. Of course, the really smart, rich and good-looking ones get to become federal ministers of the Crown, premiers and corporate hot dogs – and so can afford high-priced flacks, spin doctors and fart catchers (see Glossary) to screw up their dealings with the media for them. But until this book was written, most would-be politicians, like you, had to screw up all by themselves.

Anyway, if you're running for any office, no matter how unimportant (unless maybe it's to catch the bus out of town), you crave sycophantic clips and clippings. It is a law of nature, imprinted in your genes. All successful politicians are by nature shameless publicity hounds. If you are not embarrassed by such publicity hounding, as any decent person would be, you may be on your way to a successful second career in what's laughingly known in Canada as public service. At least, if you don't want to join a 12-step group and lie down until the urge to run for public office goes away, you will have to face up to the need, indeed the requirement, of manipulating the media.

Fortunately, you'll find it's almost laughably easy to do. In fact, therein lies one of the few significant dangers you'll encounter in public life, as long as you steer clear of outright criminality. It's so easy, you can get overconfident and do something truly bone-headed – like interrupting a journalist when he's telling you about his never-quite-finished Masters Degree thesis on Earl Camambert's personal grooming habits, or forgetting to invite a reporter down to campaign HQ for drinks and sticky buns on election night. That's why you need this guide: in essence, to let you know when you can view journalists and their employers with contempt (most of the time) and when you can let on (never).

One thing you don't have to worry about is that Woodward and Bernstein stuff you'll recall from the movies in the '70s. It almost never happens. It certainly never happens in Canada. The chances of even being asked a tough question by a Canadian reporter are roughly on a par with being hit by falling debris from a passing airliner's flush-a-bye chute. It can happen, but usually only by accident. Look, you're dealing with a crowd that includes people so deeply lazy they'd wash your feet with their hair for a useable press release, even if it was a couple of weeks old. And if you think the press is easy, you'll discover radio and TV are downright loose!

Also, just forget about politicians like Pierre Trudeau, who can break all the rules and not only get away with it but be loved for the effort. He could, you can't. Simple as that. No point even thinking about the reasons. If you could, you wouldn't be running for village council in Manyberries or Telkwa, or school board in Manitouwadge. Right? (No offence to those ably run communities.) Right.

Of course, for underfunded political novices, it is important to remember that the most effective media manipulation techniques are denied to you until you hold elective office. Consider the matter of feeding and watering the press, for example. For now, you'll have to pay for coffee and pretend you think the journalist you're begging for air or ink wouldn't stoop to taking a free lunch. Of course, once you've got an expense account, not to mention a salary, you can start pouring on the steak and lobster to wonderful effect.

The fundamental objective of this guidebook is to provide the straight goods on how to successfully manipulate the media, not the kind of laundered anodyne platitudes usually found in textbooks on public relations. Some readers will no doubt suspect that this is little more than the hyperbolic ravings of an embittered hack desperate to see his name on the spine of a book, any book. This is, of course, true. Nevertheless, the contents are also the truth, and nothing but. (see Warning.)

For most of the past two decades and more, I have been either a journalist or a practitioner of what is euphemistically known as "media relations " – that is, paid, full-time media manipulation. Media manipulation is one half of the great field of public relations. The other half is going over the head of the media to manipulate the public directly. I have dined with panic-stricken flacks who only get paid when toadying stories about their clients appear in the media; I have bought lunches for pathetic hacks who would sell their first-born children for a three-minute ride in the company helicopter. So you can trust me. This is how it is done, how the media is actually manipulated, in real life, right here in Canada.

The trouble with normal public relations guidebooks is that, first, they are usually written by people whose only association with the working media was a summer job on a community weekly 35 years ago, hence they don't know shinola from the other stuff. Second, their authors are mostly engaged in trying to persuade themselves and their clients that they're highly skilled professionals, like neurosurgeons and $1-million-a-minute drug lawyers.

This book has a more humble aim. It seeks simply to be a useful and practical guide to small-time politicians and wannabe politicians, to provide them with advice that actually works. As such, it should also be helpful to quite a broad range of undesirables, parasites and lowlifes in public and private life.

So c'mon, folks: buy the book, file your nomination papers, quit worrying, settle down and read on. . . .

Basic Media Manipulation

1

Getting Ready to Manipulate

Most novice politicians are doomed to screw up their relations with the news media, doing incalculable harm to their aspirations to high office. You don't have to mess up.

So, you want to run for an insignificant elected office?

Excellent! Even before you're elected, the first thing you're going to want to do is hold a news conference.

Trouble is, holding a news conference is probably the last thing you should actually do.

I know, I know: You've been daydreaming about it for months. There you are, in a sharp new dark suit, silk-repp tie knotted elegantly, coolly fielding questions from respectful reporters. The reporters are all well-dressed too. Some even wear expensive-looking bow-ties; others have studious and rather delicate wire-rimmed spectacles. They introduce themselves politely, in such precise phrases as: "Bert Gronk, *Punkydoodle Corners News-Advertiser....*" That dewy-eyed newscaster from Channel 9, the one with the long dark curls who used to be a beauty queen in Utah looks at you with frank interest, cheeks flushing a little and ample bosom heaving beneath her crisply tailored suit . . . or maybe it's the silver-haired airline-pilot-type that she's teamed up with that gets your little heart going pitter patter. Whatever.

Either way. . . . Get a grip!

For crying out loud, you're running for alderman in some dinky, dusty and undoubtedly nasty little place that's almost certainly well off the cultural, if not the actual, beaten path. If you were running for Mayor of Toronto or Member of Parliament, you wouldn't have to buy a book like this to learn how to tie your shoelaces, would you? In fact, you may not even be running for anything as consequential as alderman! You may be taking aim at something as breathtakingly insignificant as school trustee, summer village councillor, community association president, or block watch captain! Pierre Trudeau (remember him?) once said MPs were nobodies if they wandered further than 500 yards from Parliament Hill. *You* haven't even been elected dog catcher! Face it, right now, you don't have to walk 50 feet.

And you want to hold a news conference? If you do, let me tell you what will almost certainly happen: nobody will come. That's right, NOBODY WILL COME. You'll rent a conference room at the Sleepytime Inn, lay on sticky buns and coffee (including decaf, silly person), phone all the local newspapers, radio and television stations, and . . . nobody will turn up.

You'll stand around feeling foolish and sweaty in the cheap blue suit you bought from Mr. Big 'n' Tall or Serena or wherever you shop, clutching a pile of press releases you photocopied for full price at your brother-in-law's stupid shop. And if you've brought your spouse or kids, you'll start to burn with humiliation – as will they if they love you. You'll soon be wondering whether you should start grazing on your own sticky buns. (Well, the answer to that one is easy: What the heck, you paid for them. Like the decaf, they probably came dear, too.)

You may have noticed a guy who looked a bit like that new reporter from the community weekly come padding down the hall, take a shifty look around to see if anyone else was there, confirm that there wasn't, then slip away as discreetly as possible for a guy wearing an unfashionably wide maroon polyester necktie with embossed fleur-de-lys, a frayed shirt, a cheap blue sports coat three sizes too big, brown trousers and white high-top running shoes. You know, the one who kinda looked like he might've cut his own hair a couple of months back. Not at all like those Ivy Leaguers in your overheated fantasy, alas. And no sign of the fine-looking team from Channel 9. No chance, buddy!

And a no-show "newser" like this could turn out to be lucky. That's right, because if it's a *really* slow news day you might attract a crowd after all. Only instead of asking respectful questions preceded by their names and titles, the reporters will stand around wisecracking, saying remarkably rude things within earshot of your spouse. They'll stuff your donuts into their faces, then talk to each other with their mouths full while you try to read the "platform statement" you stayed up all night to draft. Most of them will be radio reporters from Country & Western stations, wearing red golf shirts with rubber-like stations' logos ironed on to them. And if they sense that you're overreaching – like the unemployed house-painter in a big Canadian city who decided to announce one fine, slow summer's day that he was going to run for mayor – they'll do snide little stories that purposely make you look like a dope. Especially if you slip, as the unfortunate painter did, and reveal that you have to work Ladies' Nites as a male "exotic dancer" in a local strip club to keep bread and beans on the table.

The Herding Instinct

Ironically, by holding a news conference before the time is right, you will have done one of the very, very few things you could as an aspiring politician – or aspiring anything else for that matter – to tempt news reporters to give you negative publicity. This is because, generally speaking, while often extremely lazy, reporters are horrible in groups. This is especially so if they work for inconsequential small-town radio stations or newspapers – precisely the kind of journalists you are most likely going to find yourself dealing with unless you commit an indictable offense. On their own, they are typically meek and so consistently lazy that they are powerfully inclined to pretty much say what you want them to. After all, that's one heck of a lot less work than trying to put together an expose on male politicians who, in real life, table dance for drunken hausfraus. But in a mob, all their insecurities about their low pay and lack of social status quickly blossom, and they start acting up and showing off to each other like a play-school class of four-year-olds on its first outing. This can quickly translate into extremely bad press. So, all in all, it's a good thing that they'll almost certainly have something more important to do the day an unknown novice politician like you selects to make a big announcement.

Now, there is one way these typical journalistic characteristics can accidentally lead to a dangerous misunderstanding among inexperienced office seekers. Suppose, for example, it's started to rain outside, and that fellow in the high-top sneakers didn't bring enough cash for breakfast. (Not an unusual occurrence in his case, as you can imagine.) In such circumstances, that truckload of sticky rolls you laid on may suddenly begin to beckon to him irresistibly, more powerfully even than the journalistic herd instinct that would normally repel him from a hotel conference room bereft of other reporters to stand around and shoot the breeze with. As a result, you may get *one* reporter at your news conference.

This is, in fact, extremely good luck, though it is seldom recognized as such. As a result, it can quickly turn into extremely bad luck, as we shall see. Chances are, in such circumstances, the fellow or young woman will behave as respectfully as his or her upbringing permits, ask the very polite questions you had dreamed about (although not while demonstrating the sartorial elegance and social *savoir faire* you may have imagined), use a serviette to wipe away the crumbs, and go away to write a properly deferential little story. This can lead those new to the game of politics to mistakenly conclude that they would have received five or six such positive stories had five or six reporters turned up. This, in turn, leads into temptation – making the urge to foolishly call another news conference extremely difficult to deny.

Do Not Attempt a Second News Conference!

Not, at any rate, without professional assistance. Better yet, call no second news conference until you have actually been elected to something. Should you have had the remarkable good fortune to have only one reporter show up at a premature news conference that you have injudiciously called, especially if the results have appeared in print, count your blessings. Capitalize on the fluke by sending out a news release with a photocopy of the friendly puff-piece attached. This way, you can benefit from the herd instinct entrenched in genes of most journalists, rather than be victimized by it. Remember, the fear of publishing a negative report when a positive trend has been established, runs deep among journalists.

Nevertheless, it is also important to keep in mind that your news conference fantasy is not entirely a bad thing. It clearly indicates that – on an instinctive level, at any rate – you have got one thing right about running for public office. That is, that without publicity you are as dead as a mackerel. Your daydreams show that you intuitively sense this important fact. And – unless you're a jug-eared American billionaire – you probably can't afford to pay for it.

Fending Off Questions

Don't bother spending time worrying about being thrown anything but "softball" questions. In the unlikely event you are actually asked a difficult question, you have little to fear. Simply do what all real politicians do. That is, answer another question.

There are a couple of ways to do this. If you're dealing with a newspaper or magazine reporter, you can simply plunge right into your remarks as if you are answering the question asked:

> Reporter: 'Hey, didn't I see a picture of a guy who kinda looked like you dancing Ladies' Nites at Klub Zamboanga?'
>
> You: 'I'm glad you asked that question. When I'm elected Monday, I'll see to it that every pothole in this fine community . . . blah, blah, blah'

Now, in this specific kind of case, dealing with print reporters, it often pays to go on and on – and on and on and on – until the journalist wearies of the whole affair, gives up any hope of ever asking a truly tough question and starts praying you'll just shut the heck up.

Use of this technique poses more of dilemma, however, when dealing with broadcast journalists. That is because there are also great benefits to be gained by speaking in pithy – hence hard to edit – "30-second clips," a technique that will be discussed at greater length later. So, do you speak concisely, in the hopes a particular 30-second verbal burst will prove irresistible and untouchable to a tape editor, or do you blather on and grind into submission any reporters inclined to ask you hard-to-answer questions? The choice is yours. Of course, either way there are risks. But my advice, if you're presented with an opportunity in the form of a favorable question, is to blather without mercy when you're dealing with either newspaper reporters or hard-to-control mobs of journalists who at any moment may start showing off to each other. But opt for more precise clips when facing only one or two members of the so-called "electronic media," most of whom wouldn't know a difficult question if it ran up barking and bit them on the hind-quarters.

Most big-time mayors and cabinet ministers use the unstoppable babble approach during those impromptu gang interviews known in Canadian journalism as "scrums" (named after the similarly sweaty and incoherent rugby manoeuvre). To really destroy a news conference using this technique, of course, it's best to have a flunky in tow. Then when, God willing, some sycophant from a local all-talk radio station asks the inevitable toadying question in the first 30 seconds of the scrum, the mayor or minister will just go on answering the same question without taking a breath until his loyal fart-catcher glances at his $15,000 Rolex and announces: "Sorry guys, time's up! Gotta plane to catch." Master and servant immediately stride off, ignoring the shouts and pleas of any anguished reporters who actually had real questions to ask. If broadcasters are present, of course, the correct form is to summarize the first reporter's fawning question in even more favorable form, then answer the rephrased question. Since a typical radio or TV news segment is only about three nanoseconds long anyway, chances are there won't be time to play the reporter ponderously intoning his only slightly less favorable version of the same question.

Needless to say, faced with a genuinely probing question, this approach MUST be used without hesitation.

> Reporter: 'What are you going to do now that council's interest-free loan to your brother-in-law's photocopy shop has completely destroyed the village budget?'

> You: 'Good question, Bob. You've asked me what we can do to bring even more economic opportunities to our village. . . .'

Indeed, your ability to effortlessly engage in this fundamentally dishonest rhetorical technique is probably as good a test as any of your suitability for politics. Scientists believe most successful politicians are born with a gene that makes them ignore questions and answer other queries they weren't asked.* Should

---

* I just made up this part, sorry.

you actually start to forthrightly answer hard questions from reporters (or your spouse, for that matter), especially if you repeat their loaded phrases or unintentionally behave in any other honest or honorable manner, it may be evidence you are genetically unsuited to politics.

A better question to be asking yourself as you ponder a political career might be: "How can I keep from looking like a total jackass?"

There is always the risk that any reporter who bothers to show up to interview you will miss anything really stupid that you say and just let the tapes roll unedited. This is seldom done out of malice, though it's been known to happen. Usually the cause is pure laziness, or a genuine inability to understand what you're talking about.

So, for starters, the onus is entirely on you to make sure you don't stuff your foot in your mouth. And, face it, you've already got a problem not looking like a dope if you're one of 25 or 30 candidates who's just slapped down $100 you could have invested in something sensible like lottery tickets to run in, say, an aldermanic by-election.

An excellent starting point for your effort to avoid looking pathetically idiotic is avoid all jokes – no matter how hilarious – that poke fun at women, sexual predilections, other races, or which tell about a priest, a rabbi and a minister together in an airplane that's just run out of fuel. This is especially true if tapes are running anywhere in the vicinity.* Likewise, never describe sexual activity of any sort. However, pithy descriptions of animal excrement are acceptable, if used to make a point in a down-home manner that shows you, like Ross Perot, to be a stand-up guy: " 'Mericans are just gonna hafta muck out th' barn. . . . "

Of course, as illustrated above, the most important contribution you can make to not looking foolish in public is to eschew holding news conferences until you have actually been elected to something.

---

* They always are, nowadays.

In the meantime, you still need to get the media to treat you as if you are a serious and thoughtful individual, the kind of person whose self-serving pronouncements are regurgitated without hesitation* or thought. This requires understanding, especially on your part, of how the media works.

---

* It has been reported in the public prints (for what it is worth) that studies indicate that politicians that intersperse their talk with "uhs" and pauses are often misconstrued by the public as hiding the truth, even though the average person uses "uh" frequently in conversation. Hence the prevalence of what sounds like rehearsed answers from most "smooth-talking" politicians.

2

Understanding the Media

The biggest mistake most political aspirants make is letting their contempt for the media show.

*I*t is hardly front-page news that the media in the modern English-speaking world is nowadays widely viewed as a thoroughly contemptible institution.

All the big players act as if this were true – beneficiaries, victims and participants alike. Viewers and readers pick up on it and assume it as a matter of course. Heck, this must be true! The media's own polling consistently shows journalists rank somewhere between used-computer salespeople and television evangelists on the public's faith-and-trust meter.

So what? On its own, this isn't particularly useful or startling information. But in the wrong hands – like those of a striver after the most insignificant political office – it has the potential to be disastrous.

How so? Because an inchoate feeling of deep contempt for the media – even if justified – can lead you into dangerous waters. ("Shark-infested waters," as we inevitably say in journalese.) It may tempt you, in other words, to treat the media with the contempt you think it deserves.

This is hardly prudent, yet it is quite remarkable how many blunder into precisely this type of behavior.

Now, naturally, most carping about the media is merely the whingeing of quite-properly-zinged ne'er-do-wells. Still, it is true that, despite the best intentions of most of the people who work there, many of the media's wounds are self-inflicted. Understanding the media's many failings is essential to anyone who hopes to launch a successful career in politics, for, properly put to work, such knowledge can be the key to effortless and effective media manipulation.

That, obviously, is the principal objective of everyone in public life.

It is an easy objective because, alas, in the late 20th century it can be said of more journalistic enterprises than it cannot that they are lazy, illiterate, timid, reactive, devoid of rational discourse and, for the most part, deservedly going broke. (Fortunately for me, I work for one of the exceptions, else I couldn't pen a snotty tome like this.)

Existential Leads (Bad Writing 101)

Most news businesses, like all large enterprises, are distinguished by a rigidly conventional approach to doing their daily routine, and a stiflingly bureaucratic mindset that recoils in horror and fear at the contemplation of anything resembling originality.

For instant evidence, look no farther than the "existential lead." You may never have heard this particular term for this trite and irritating journalistic trick. Indeed, it is a locution seldom used by journalists, especially those most inclined to use the technique. Nevertheless, despite its lack of currency in the argot of the trade, the existential lead is beloved of newspapers, even good ones, everywhere that English is spoken. Indeed, you will recognize this depressing opening gambit the moment you have the misfortune to stumble upon an example.

Long or short, existential leads are always written in the present tense. A story beginning with an existential lead paragraph goes like this:

> They sit in class in wheelchairs with their hands taped to simulate arthritis. Nurses come in and start spooning Jell-O into their mouths.

I'm not making any of this up; this is an actual existential lead, selected at random from a recent edition of a real Canadian daily newspaper. Quite a good one, as a matter of fact. Which proves, I guess, that bad writing can even appear in good newspapers. Here's another example from the same publication:

> William is slumped half conscious in the back seat of the van. . .

In case a reader had any doubts about finishing this gem, its author went on:

> . . . between hiccups, he froths at the mouth. His eyes roll and his chin drops to his chest with a groan.

Your chin will drop to your chest with a groan, too, if you ever read another existential lead.

What is the reaction of the normal, red-blooded Canadian reader when he or she comes upon an existential lead? Precisely the same as yours – extreme and debilitating boredom. In an instant, the reader's eye sends a signal to the brain . . . "BOR-RING" . . . the brain flashes a message back to the eye; the restless eye moves on.

You don't actually *think* that an existential lead is a surefire sign of a pointless, uninteresting, uninformative and generally irrelevant story. (What is generally known in the newspaper business as "a good read.") You just *know* it. As when your finger senses heat, the reaction is instant, instinctive and impossible to deny.

So why do so many newspapers persist, even as the red ink slops across so many of their decks, in pressing on with a formula so whacked-out that almost everyone outside the business intuitively gags at it on sight? It's simple. It's been done before!

Isn't this what social scientists call "consensus anonymity?" That is, when everybody does exactly the same thing all of the time, because obviously it must be a good idea if everybody's doing it. Also, more importantly, no one can get in trouble for doing it again. Bureaucratic consensual anonymity is driven by the same timorous instinct, one supposes, that makes North American television hosts interrupt their guests whenever they (the guests, that is) are in danger of saying something interesting.

It is certainly what drives many large news media businesses to unremittingly persist in a thousand and one trite and pointless gimmicks from uninteresting human-interest stories, to indecipherable graphs, to choosing bad wire news over good local reporting, to ubiquitous "women's columns" (and, now, God help us, "sensitive men's" columns!), to ceaselessly replaying the uninformed and usually idiotic ramblings of persons encountered by camera crews wandering the streets. (Extremely small media operations, by the way, are usually run by authoritarian but quite-unbureaucratic cranks. Unfortunately, however, since these cranks are usually the embittered products of more bureaucratic media enterprises, their eccentricity seldom amounts to much.)

How could such self-destructive behavior have become the norm? I personally think it is the result of the amazing fact that for almost a century up to, oh, say 10 or 15 years ago, one could do virtually anything one wanted while running a newspaper and still make pots of money. When radio and television came along, the same rule applied with a vengeance. As a result, now that we have finally reached a point in history where technology and social change have conspired to make media businesses less automatically profitable (aka, the Internet), many in the industry are hamstrung by a century of bad ideas turned into unshakable traditions.

As readers and viewers file quietly to the lifeboats, the result among many people in charge of media enterprises is panic and inertia. This seems to be as true of large companies as small ones. And, when this happens, journalists naturally become increasingly bureaucratic. After all, bureaucracy is no different in a large international media and entertainment conglomerate than it is in the governments and other big businesses journalists are always writing heavy-breathing editorials about. To wit: The principal objective of all bureaucracies is to enable the bureaucrats operating within to evade all responsibility for their actions. By becoming more bureaucratic and cautious, news managers and journalists hope to shield themselves from responsibility for the financial catastrophe facing many of their employers.

Consider this any time your favorite news program or newspaper does something that makes absolutely no sense from the point of view of speedily providing accurate and up-to-date information or running a profitable business. For a quick explanation that does make sense, ask: Might some bureaucratic objective be achieved by this senseless occurrence?

The upshot of this state of affairs is that nearly all news stories in the media sound the same, all news pictures look the same, all film clips sound and look the same, all opinion columns venture the same opinions, and all events require the same brainless "reaction."

But the point of this sermon about the collective failings of so much of the media is that this presents you, the aspiring politician or other publicity hound, with a priceless opportunity. And nowhere is this better demonstrated than with the unbreakable, unbendable, institutional law that for every news story there must be an equal and opposite reaction.

Recording those Reactions

Like a lot of truly bad ideas, there's enough sense to this one to make it really dangerous. Obviously, reaction to a news story is justified and fair in some cases. For example, it's a reasonable principle that when really horrible charges are levelled in print or on the air at someone in public life, they should have the opportunity to respond:

> Public Decency Minister Elmo Skrunk is a 'despicable human being' who has fathered 17 illegitimate children, Opposition decency critics said. . . .
>
> 'What a terrible thing to say about innocent little babies who have committed no crime but to be born without a man around the house to give 'em a last name,' Skrunk responded later in the day as he left Parliament Hill.

(Of course, if you're not in public life, and you don't have access to your own pet journalists, you're probably out of luck in this specific kind of situation.)

But this sensible principle becomes ludicrous when bureaucracy and habit decree that reporters must seek out a reaction comment to *every* story that they run, i.e., "Members of the city's Kruk Islander community said they were 'upset' and 'distressed' at reports a volcano completely destroyed their homeland moments before it sank into the Pacific Ocean." I mean, for heaven's sake, you'd be distressed and upset too, if Mom, Pop, Cousin Akhmud, your boyhood friend Tamu the Rescue Dog, not to mention the beach-front property on which you'd planned to spend a pleasant and well-lubricated retirement had just disappeared beneath the roiling, shark-infested waters of the Pacific! Consider another perennial reaction favorite:

Meanwhile, Canadian Legion officials in the Vancouver Island village of Peckerwood decried as 'regrettable' charges their campaign to keep men in turbans and beanies out of their beer parlour is motivated by racism.

Nosiree Bob! Just worried they'll start conducting worship services that don't involve the use of Molson's draft as a sacrament.

How does this reaction reflex benefit you, the would-be alderman or school trustee? Obviously, it gives you liberal opportunities to provide such reaction, hence it gets your name on the air or in print as often as is humanly possible. Now, if you're really serious about politics, you'll want to be sure to make yourself available at any time of night or day, no matter how inconvenient, to do this. Because, after all, if you're new at this game you're generally not going to be the first choice for a comment. If you're willing to provide a comment on any topic regardless of the hour, however, the word will soon go out in the fraternity (sorority?) of hacks and hackettes that you are a dependable source of sound quotes. The benefits of this recognition are potentially enormous, and your name should soon be popping up in the media with gratifying regularity.

Don't Become a "Rent-A-Mouth"

However, if possible, you may want to try to avoid going so far with this that you become what is known in the trade as an outright "rent-a-mouth" – that is, someone so promiscuous with quotes that he or she becomes an object of mockery. Still, given the choice early in your career of being held up to ridicule for saying too much, or simply saying too little in the media, it is clearly better to suffer the scorn of being classified as a rent-a-mouth. After all, in politics, having your name recognized is nine-tenths of the battle. Oscar Wilde still says it best: "Better to be spoken of badly than not to be spoken of at all."

Obviously, if you make yourself a rent-a-mouth or just generally available for comments, you'll be called upon from time to time to deal with some genuinely controversial topics like the right of certain people to exclude certain others from their Legion beer halls and other places of worship. When this happens, you'll want to ensure that your comments are as anodyne as possible: "I'm certainly for freedom of expression, and freedom generally, because I'm a big believer in people, but I think we've all got to get together as a community to work out some sort of reasonable compromise here. . . ."

If you are serious about becoming a politician, you should have no qualms whatsoever about phoning up local reporters and offering comments on anything under the sun. Naturally, your comments will not always be used, and you shouldn't be hurt when they aren't. But you will be pleasantly surprised how often they do get on to the air or into print when no one better than you can be rounded up for comment. This is especially true with stories that break late in the day.

It may also be helpful to develop some area of bogus expertise. If your day job involves selling insurance or mutual funds, for example, you should always make an effort to flog comments on investment or insurance questions facing council or the school board. (This can also serve as free advertising if you don't manage to get elected.) You can and should feel free to stretch this principle as far as possible. If your hobby is model railroading, for example, and your basement contains an extensive HO-gauge model of the Pacific Great Eastern switching yards in Prince George, you are obviously qualified to comment on any or all transportation issues facing any level of government. By the same token, if you have a wife or children or know anyone who does, you are entirely within your rights to comment on questions pertaining to sex or drugs. Provided, of course, that you advocate neither.

Finally, in the absence of any Kruk Islanders, you should never hesitate to express sympathy or to promise efforts to assist the victims of natural disasters anywhere in the south seas – indeed, anywhere outside the nastiest corners of the Middle East.

This, in turn, leads us to another common news media foible that is ready made for the aspiring politician. That is, "the local angle." Some media operations carry this to extremes – *"Two Local Women Missing! South Korea completely destroyed in Earthquake"* – but all feel obliged to practice it to some extent.

So keep a card file of all ethnic, religious, military veterans', trade and hobby groups that you know of. Should some misfortune befall any of them or their loved ones, be sure to try to appear at a news conference with them to offer support/sympathy/a public-spirited shoulder to sob upon. Again, this is a good example of a time when you can effectively get in touch with the media. "Say, Darlene, I know you've been following the meltdown at the former Lenin Reactor in Omsk. . . . Well, I just happen to know a young refugee fellow whose family still lives right over the border in Ukraine. Actually, it's a couple of hundred miles, but . . ."

If, through the use of gambits like this, you are successful in becoming the bottomless well of quotable quotes you need to be to really get ahead in politics, you will need to hone the now well-developed media manipulation technique, the "30-second clip."

30-Second Clips

The 30-second clip is essentially the verbal form of a news release – that is, a spoken quote for broadcasters so lucid and self contained no editor or reporter dares to tamper with it. (So vital are news releases as a media manipulation technique that the next chapter is devoted to the topic in its entirety.) It is not the proper response to every situation – flight or filibuster work better in the face of sustained, hostile questioning. But as a way of manipulating radio and television interviewers, it is without parallel.

It is a fact little understood by outsiders (who often imagine that the opposite is true), that television above all is the easiest medium of news to manipulate. Radio reporters are a little better situated to fend off the grossest sorts of manipulation, though not much. And while hardly ambitious in this regard, the press as a class has the most time and inclination to analyze and comment upon events instead of just regurgitating contrived quotes. This is why the press is hated the most by professional politicians.

When it comes to television, there are three main reasons for this phenomenon: lack of time, the absolute requirement for visual material, and the poor general quality of broadcast reporters. First, the ability to meet deadlines every hour on the hour is the reason broadcasters have become the pre-eminent source of news for most human beings on the planet. Unfortunately, the pressure of constant deadlines seldom leaves broadcast journalists with enough time to do their jobs properly even if they could. Second, television reporters must spend hours travelling to buildings, large objects and disaster sites to stand in front of them. Time that could be spent actually reporting, or even profitably making interesting personal phone calls, is frittered away on the silly notion the reporter must always be seen standing before the topic of the report. Third, television reporters are chosen for their looks, not their brains. Hence, many are quite dumb. (This may also explain why newspaper journalists – present company excepted, of course – are seldom all that good looking.)

As a result, television news organizations are natural victims for a media manipulator willing to be interviewed on camera standing in front of something large. This is especially so if he or she can deliver pithy, to-the-point (usually misleading and always self-serving) 30-second clips. You can practice making these bright little speeches in front of the bathroom mirror. Imagine yourself being asked a tough question. Then repeat a 30-second answer to another question.

While we are on the topic of the delivery of 30-second clips, let us consider for a moment the related matter of the Queen's English.

Although one, of course, strives in 30 seconds to make one's points clearly, and in a manner that is as hard as possible to edit, it is by no means necessary (or even desirable) to speak like a hoity-toity music reviewer for a little magazine of the arts, a school teacher or even a modestly educated and well-spoken working person. On the contrary, a certain amount of bad grammar and the occasional amusing malapropism will endear you to the press and public alike. So do not cast asparagus upon those politicians who fail to use proper English. It may well contribute to their success. As for broadcast journalists, they probably won't even notice, speaking, as they do, that way themselves.

This is not to say that you should resort to profanity or obscenity — spicing your conversation with effin' this and effin' that, this will identify you a little to effin' closely for comfort with the effin' public that you hope will vote for you. (They don't mind it in their movie stars, but let's face it you aren't auditioning for a movie.) But judicious use of the occasional "ain't," "youse," or goofball mispronunciation will likely not, to paraphrase a successful and well-known Member of Parliament from Western Canada, cause nobody to hold no animation against ya.

In other words, hurling an epitaph now and then may put out your back, but it is likely to do little harm with voters, and it will surely endear you to many journalists — who will give you ink and air time out of gratitude for the colorful quotes.

Obviously, these and many other of the media's myriad weak points can be easily turned to your advantage. In fact, you will find the news media often embarrassingly easy to manipulate. Indeed, with each passing day — as more media workers conclude the path to success lies in the cautious spinning of red tape not in aggressive reporting — it gets easier. Still, the critical lesson remains: Do not let practitioners of journalism see your contempt for their craft, even if entirely justified.

Don't Call Reporters Jerks

Let's face it, nobody likes being told you think they're a jerk. And for those bright enough to recognize what's going on around them, few appreciate hearing suggestions they've screwed up a perfectly reasonable life during which they could have just as easily gone to law school and have been adequately compensated for enduring the public's contempt. Yet that, no matter how legitimate your scorn, is precisely what you're doing when you let some poor underpaid journalistic hack listen to a symphonized version of the BeeGees for 45 minutes of telephonic hold while your beautiful Malaysian pedicurist blows your freshly polished toenails dry. You can be sure that the reporter is acutely aware of both the lack of funds and social status that this wait signifies.

You see, while many reporters are quite possibly as dumb as stumps, some are actually fairly bright, and a few even entered the field with honorable intentions. But except for a few stars in the small number of top jobs in an equally small number of elite organizations – usually a former network president's son, someone who isn't going to die for a long, long time – most eventually come to realize that they've made a profoundly wrong-headed career decision. While less bright, or at least less facile, classmates begin turning up as contented and prosperous ambassadors, lawyers and captains of industry, a lot of reasonably intelligent reporters are left to the slowly dawning knowledge that life isn't going to be the effortless literary romp they had expected.

Suddenly feeling like a chiropodist at a convention of podiatric surgeons, or an optometrist who's accidentally booked passage on an ophthalmologists' cruise, the guy you're about to put down may be looking for a toe to step on or an eye to poke. If you blunder on to the political scene dripping with contempt for journalists, you may make a highly desirable target for such a reporter's professional frustrations. (Remember, at the moment you are likely a complete unknown, except perhaps within the Moose Lodge or the Legion beer parlor! Hence, this is possibly the most vulnerable moment in your electoral career.)

So treat the reporters with whom you must deal with simple good manners and common decency. The gesture may not be appreciated, or even recognized. But it's better than the alternative. Just remember, you don't have to personally like a mugger to see the wisdom of quietly handing over your wallet.

However, should it simply become impossible to suppress any longer a public expression of your contempt for the media, at least consider prudently the choice of your target. Here your strategy should be the opposite of the best approach to suing for defamation (see Chapter 8). That is to say, there's generally less risk in lambasting the big guys than taking on the little guy just down the block. This is not to say the little guy is tougher, only that he's going to be around more (and probably longer) to do you harm.

Yet given the opportunity, most novice politicians get this principle exactly backwards, to their everlasting grief. Naturally, they are complimented and pleased if they're approached for a comment by some big-shot reporter from Toronto. The kid from the *Weekly Advertiser* is familiar to the point of contempt. But consider, who can really hurt you, council meeting after council meeting, week after week? The guy from Toronto will have forgotten about you five minutes after he's filed his story, no matter what you said about his mother. Not so Johnny of the *Advertiser*. So if kick you must, why not kick the butt of Mr. Hotshot-in-the-bow-tie? For weeks everyone will admire your courage. Even the kid from the local rag will say a silent prayer of thanks and maybe go easy on you the next couple of times you goof up.

Better, though, to be nice to all comers. Just remember, bad as the news media's reputation may be, it's better than it once was. A lot of people *do* believe what they read in the newspaper, and a majority believe what they see on TV (because, poor delusional fools, they think since they saw it with their own eyes that the image couldn't have been manipulated). So just keep your contempt to yourself!

NOTE: Not a word of the foregoing should be construed to suggest that you should address members of the news media in Canada by anything but their first names. It is the custom in Canada for reporters to address politicians and senior bureaucrats respectfully by their last names and honorifics, or better yet by their titles. Officials, by contrast, are expected to respond to reporters, no matter how exalted, by their first names, preferably diminutives. "Just a minute Bob, I think Janey is asking a question. . . ." Respect, after all, is all very well, but not at the expense of losing the proper perspective on the pecking order.

3

Dressing For Political Success

Looking sharp may work. Not looking sharp may work
more often. Why you should not take advice on what to
wear from journalists, present company excepted.

What could be more pathetic than a grown man in a nice dark new suit and a pair of white high-top sneakers? The same man running for public office in that getup, that's what.

I can offer no insights into why would-be political office holders in Canada so often commit this particular sartorial sin. Indeed, it seems to be a topic largely ignored by sociologists and political scientists. I can only advise – should you be tempted to run for office so clad – that you ought not to.

Oddly, it is worth noting, that women in politics – indeed, women in general – can often get away with wearing sneakers on such occasions. This is because anyone nowadays who sees a woman in a smart businesslike costume and a pair of canvas running shoes will assume that she's a careerist yuppie getting fit by walking to the subway as all those women's magazines are forever recommending. And since virtually all women running for public office of late are, in fact, careerist yuppies, even in cities that don't have subways, such an approach to dressing can prove less harmful than it might to a man. Still, canvas or rubber shoes, especially at a woman candidate's first news conference, are best complemented by a leg cast and a pair of crutches. Under all circumstances, moreover, women who aspire to be taken seriously in any circle should eschew the kind of footwear popular among ladies of the evening. For the same reason, unjust though popular prejudices about cosmetics may be, serious female candidates should as a general rule avoid wearing deep scarlet lipstick or black fingernail varnish. Unless, of course, you are running for the presidency of the Elvira Impersonators Society.

Scandals – I Mean Sandals

Getting back to the politics of footwear, if you're a man, you should avoid sandals. For some reason, men who wear sandals seem to have difficulty attaining political office in Canada. Personally, I believe it has something to do with the strong sentiments felt by many members of the public about whether socks should, or should not, be worn with that particular type of shoe. Wear 'em, and you're certain to offend somebody. Don't, ditto! Likewise, if you're male, female or anything else and are going to succeed at a run for public office, chances are virtually certain that you're going to have to do a lot of walking from door to door, so even if you happen to be that one-in-a-million individual who can pull off wearing cowboy boots or pumps with four-inch heels while still maintaining an air of dignity and credibility, at the end of the day your feet are going to hurt like the dickens. So why not avoid both political danger and sore feet by opting for a sensible pair of walking shoes that'll go with either business clothes or bluejeans?

Which brings us in passing to another vital point about running for office in Canada. If you're a middle-aged white male – and chances are if you're running for alderman, anyway, that you are – you should not take the expression literally. That is to say, unless you're that extremely rare natural athlete, don't – repeat, *do not* – actually run from door to door when campaigning. If you can barely restrain yourself, sit down for a moment and recall what an absolute moron Joe Clark looked like when the TV cameras caught *him* jogging from door to door. Then, *walk*!

Incidentally, to my fellow journalists, I advise that you *do not* – *ever* – volunteer to comment on women's clothing unless you are a woman, or a fashion consultant, or have been forced to, as I have been, by the editor of this guidebook.* Since I started in the news business nearly a quarter of a century ago, I have only once been threatened with death and that was for writing about how women dress. The specific threat, no doubt from a fellow completely fed up with listening to his wife or girlfriend natter on about my literary wickedness, was to cut me in half with a chainsaw if I wrote another word about *haute couture*. Now, this took place in Prince Rupert, British Columbia, where – for heaven's sake – all I did was point out that the ladies of that fine northern port city, where I then resided, did not dress as

---

* There are some who might question the wisdom of such a request, given that yours truly in 1974 was runner-up for the uncoveted title of worst-dressed reporter at a well known western-Canadian daily newspaper. Who actually won is lost in the mists of time, but it's a fact that it was the unwashed, navy blue, bell-bottom trousers that clinched second place.

well as their equivalents in Paris, France. The thesis of my article for a southern newspaper was that a critical mass of fashionable people is required to properly pull off a state of being truly fashionable. I also noted that there were a lot of men in that community with really spectacularly bizarre haircuts. Well, I've learned my lesson. Except for the part about the haircuts, not a word of what I wrote was true. The women of the lower Skeena wear their gumboots with a panache unseen on the muddy banks of the Seine.

The Tailored Suit

Regardless, if you're a man and the thought has occurred to you that you can probably get away with wearing your old sneakers with your new suit, lie down till it goes away. If the urge is really strong, call somebody you trust to talk you out of it.

Now, this advice does not mean that men thinking of running for elected office should immediately drop several hundred free-floating Canadian credonias on a new pair of cordovan leather loafers to go with their new suits. On the contrary, male and female political novices alike may be wise to consider hanging up their new suits and campaigning in the clothes they normally wear.

After all, the point of dressing for political success is to look like a credible candidate. What many novice politicians, as they dream about their public careers to come, mistakenly conclude from this is that the people they're trying to look credible to are national news anchors and the editorial board of big daily newspapers in Toronto. In other words, the kind of people they imagine worry about things like how political candidates dress. (It is an irrelevant but nevertheless interesting factoid that members of the editorial board of *The Globe and Mail*, the only big Toronto newspaper that this author has ever had the privilege of working for, generally dress like street people or, worse, CBC producers. If this supposed audience was in fact the real one, then it might be reasonable to conclude that a nice suit and a silk-repp tie – or whatever the feminine equivalent of that useless item of clothing is – would be just the ticket.)

But in reality, the people a politician really needs to look credible to are the voters.

In other words, if you're thinking of running for school trustee or alderman – and not something like President of the United States of America or secretary-general of the United Nations – the people most likely to vote for you in most Canadian communities aren't likely to be the kind of people who routinely wear $3,000 five-piece suits with sleeve buttons that actually work, or for that matter delicate little Givenchy frocks. On the contrary, most of them probably wear stretch bluejeans and high-tops.

Which leads us to Dave's First Law of Political Dressing: "Dress like the folks you expect to vote for ya." Dress down, and you probably won't get elected. Dress up, and you're virtually certain not to. To put this another way: don't dump the sneakers, hang up the suit.

This advice probably doesn't hold, of course, if you happen to be a rich toff. But, then, if you are, you probably wouldn't buy this book anyway; and, if you did, you wouldn't take its advice if you could pay more for worse advice from someone else. So go fly a kite!

Anyway, it's almost certainly true that you already dress like the people who are most likely to vote for you. So you've probably already got the clothes you'll require for a successful run at public office. What's more, you won't feel at ease in a fancy suit if you're used to wearing something with your first name stitched on the sleeve, so every time you meet some actual voters, it'll make you look about as comfortable as a Jehovah's Witness in a blood-donor clinic – which the typical Canadian elector will ascribe to the reasonable likelihood that you're a liar and a thieving crook. If you manage to finagle an appearance on television, you'll look even more uncomfortable – and hence even more crooked – thanks to that medium's tendency to focus on and exaggerate any slight personal tics or physical oddities (which is also, as noted above, why you shouldn't ever be caught jogging during an election campaign, especially if you run like you have hemorrhoids).

So stick with clothes you're used to.

Frumps in Fashion

And while sticking with your old clothes, I believe credible political candidates need not be particularly worried about the kind of dressing-for-success foolishness often dispensed by ladies' magazines and those faintly disreputable publications that are aimed at clotheshorse males suffering from dispositional ambiguity. Women are advised by such publications to avoid frumpy clothes. Well fine, if that's your priority. But there's no evidence that women who look frumpy are failures in politics. On the contrary. One need look no farther than the coins in one's pocket to see a likeness of Elizabeth the Second, Queen of Canada. Not only are her relatives odious, but her garments are positively ridiculous, not to mention usually ridiculously frumpy. Yet she remains genuinely popular – even among Canadians who think having a foreign monarch as head of state is a loony anachronism. Moreover, Her Majesty's fashion equivalents enjoy continuing political popularity in every region of the land. So, obviously, avoiding female frumpiness is no formula for automatic political success. The matronly and motherly "look" just may be considered "sexy" by voters, so don't throw out your pink polka dot number, ladies, put the Donna Karan on hold.

Likewise, I believe that advice for men suggesting they ought not wear stripes or belts that exaggerate their expanding middles can be safely ignored. For heaven's sake, if overweight white guys couldn't succeed at politics, the legislative chambers of this land would be empty! Personally, I often vote for the overweight guy on the reasonable theory that any male over 40 who would spend money on a gym membership ought not to be trusted with public funds under any circumstances whatsoever. As for female candidates and obesity, whatever real or imagined reasons women as a group may have for worrying constantly about their weight, success in politics self-evidently need not be one of them. The significant number of gravitationally challenged women who are even bigger successes in the political arena proves it. Indeed, I think it may be an advantage – I suspect a lot of people who fuss needlessly and unrelentingly about their own *avoirdupois* will go out and vote for a "substantial" woman just to say "Well, bully for her!"

Moreover, with the exception of their feelings about sandals on men, Canadian voters seem willing to tolerate a remarkable degree of sartorial weirdness among their political representatives. Not only could Pierre Trudeau campaign in buckskin and succeed, but there's a female alderman I know of whose numerous re-elections have never been hampered by the fact she frequently wears a lime-green pantsuit. Such examples are legion. Oddly, however, voters appear less tolerant of tonsorial eccentricity. Since the hairless Edgar Benson left the political scene decades ago, there have been few examples of successful politicians at any level with really peculiar haircuts. (No mohawks; precious few male ponytails.) Even neatly trimmed beards and moustaches seem to make electors pretty jumpy. Ditto for earrings on men. Few explanations suggest themselves in an era when hardly a man under 50 seems to be without a moustache and an earring.

Of course, sticking with the clothes you're used to means that if you are in fact part of the crowd known in the working world as "the suits," you might as well wear one. Chances are, nobody but other suits are going to vote for you anyway, unless you have one heck of a lot to spend on advertising. On the bright, side, however, if you are a member of this set, you most likely already own a nice-looking pair of shoes, so you can keep your white sneakers in the closet with the rest of your dirty little secrets. On the other hand, though, there's plenty of evidence that even the suits won't be wearing suits much longer. "Casual Fridays" are creeping into the rest of the week, and not just at wild-eyed little software companies down in nutty northern California. No less than the mighty Ford Motor Co. of Dearborn, MI – where during the mid-1980s, when I covered the auto industry, men and women even worked in the privacy of their offices with their jackets on and their shirt collars buttoned – has decreed that all employees can dress casually all week long. So it's only a matter of time until a town council somewhere votes to let members conduct business while wearing T-shirts. The rest, even the ones with cable TV coverage, will race to follow with all the decorum of a bunch of reporters on their way to the free-beer tent.

Upgrading Your Wardrobe

Nevertheless, once elected, you may be tempted to upgrade your wardrobe. And there is a school of thought that this is a legitimate, even necessary, re-election strategy. I personally remain sceptical, however. Yes, it will be suggested to you that you'll want to expand your political base a bit, and there is some truth to this. But ask yourself honestly, isn't it really going to be basically the same bunch of suckers you're going to be going back to for re-election three or four years hence? (I can't help but recall the fate of my old college crony, who ended up briefly as a Member of Parliament for a working-class riding in the central interior of British Columbia. I foresaw his political doom the night I noticed him on national TV snipping a ribbon on a railway siding while wearing a distinguished and beautiful – nay, virtually gorgeous – pearl-grey suit. Nearby stood the local Reform party candidate, resplendent in the traditional "full Nanaimo" – white belt, sagging gut, scuffed white shoes and trousers made out of a gasoline derivative. Guess who's the MP now.)

But if fear of voters isn't enough to persuade you not to spend your hard-earned income on expensive and uncomfortable new garments, consider this: Many Canadian town and city councils, and not a few school boards, vote themselves a budget for the purchase of sharp new blue blazers immediately after being elected to a term in office. If your council hasn't yet opted to spend the taxpayers' dollars in this way, you should introduce such a motion as soon as you're elected. Your fellow councillors are trustees and sure to quickly see the wisdom of your proposal.

And a good-quality dark blazer goes fine almost anywhere. You can wear one with jeans when you're drumming up votes from the boys at the meat-packing plant without offending anyone too much (and blood splatters won't show) or you can pass it off as a formal jacket on the last night of the ocean cruise you take after the voters have cottoned on and turfed you deservedly out of office. If you can't afford the cruise, at least you can snip off your town's crest and sew on one from the Legion. So you'll always have something nice to show for your years or months in public service. And to the ladies, traditional as it may seem, if you're going to go casual, skirts are generally preferable to wearing slacks, and slacks are preferable to jeans. Don't ask me why.*

In conclusion, aside from a few obvious sartorial gaffes, like wearing a "Free Bosnia" T-shirt to an all-candidates' meeting at the Serbian Hall, "What to wear?" is a question you need not fret overmuch about while contemplating a run for public office.

The only people likely to actually pay any attention to how you dress are in the media and – uniquely on this issue – they're essentially of no account. After all, Canadians think "elite" when they think of the media as class – even if the reality of the pathetically underpaid reporters you'll actually be dealing with is quite the contrary. So, if a journalist ever actually dares to ridicule you for your clothes – or your looks, or your weight – he or she is likely doing you a favor.

Under such an attack, Canadians – fair-minded folks that they are – will most certainly vote for you out of sheer malicious spite!

And here's a thought, maybe voters care more about what you say, than what you wear?

---

* My editor made me write this. Apparently it's true?

Intermediate Media Manipulation

4

How to Write Effective
News Releases

News releases are the cornerstones of media
manipulation. How to get the publicity you want by
encouraging journalists to be lazy.

*E*ffective manipulation of the news media requires the preparation of effective news releases.

The logic behind this axiomatic truth, though seldom spoken, is impeccable: Writing effective news releases is absolutely essential because journalists as a class* are absolutely lazy.

What an effective news release does, in other words, is make it as easy as possible for reporters to get their jobs done to the satisfaction of their bosses without having to exert more than an absolute minimum amount of energy (which is most folks' natural inclination anyway). By enabling this to happen, you maximize the chances your message will be relayed to the newspaper's readers or broadcaster's audience exactly as you want it to be, with as little editorial interference or checking as possible. Since you may quite often be lying, this lack of attention can be very important, even essential.

A news release (also still sometimes termed a press release, an anachronistic term dating to the pleasant days before Country & Western radio stations employed reporters) is a short, typewritten, self-serving announcement that mimics the format of the standard "wire service news story," and hence the most common variety of newspaper story. The term, by the way, was invented by public relations types to make their work sound legitimate and important. It implies that they somehow have a right to control the flow of news. "Publicity handout" would be more accurate.

The Inverse Pyramid, 30, Bylines

Now, this is basic stuff, but let's trot through it anyway.

Wire services were what kept folks up to date about international events during the Golden Age of Print, that is, before the invention of CNN. Since, it was reasoned, individual newspapers couldn't have correspondents everywhere, they would subscribe to a wire service, which would keep them and their readers abreast of events in far-flung locales. Some wire services were

---

* Some exceptions may apply.

nominally co-operatives. That is to say, some poor underpaid hack in a usually unnewsworthy place like Moncton would write stories for the local paper, which could then be picked up by the wire service without payment to the author for use in, say, Prince Rupert. There, another hack's deathless prose could be relayed, sans royalties, back to Moncton, or anywhere else along the wire where someone had a six-column-inch hole to fill. Despite the fact there is some legitimacy to the notion one newspaper can't staff every location on the planet just because a volcano might erupt nearby at any moment, the real appeal of wire services was that they provided an extremely cheap way for large numbers of insignificant newspapers to fill the empty spaces around the advertisements.

Since lots of different newspapers with lots of different space requirements all had to be able to use the same story, articles needed to be prepared in the wire-service style, known in the trade as "the inverse pyramid." Still with us? This method of composing a news story is called an upside-down pyramid because, at least in theory, the most important stuff's at the top, and each subsequent paragraph is of decreasing importance. This way, any story can be amputated anywhere, above or below the knee, to fit any hole in any newspaper.

It goes without saying that this formula is an invitation to inelegant, not to mention uninformative, writing. From the start, however, its obvious economic benefits far outweighed its deficiencies as a communications tool. Thus wire-service style writing has become the cast-iron standard for the entire news industry.

Remarkably, even television and radio reporters stick by this formula – just watch any national newscast for proof of this assertion – even though it makes their spoken accounts of current events virtually incomprehensible. Anyone remotely familiar with spoken storytelling knows that a chronological style is likely to works best over the airwaves. But old habits die hard, especially when the old-habit holders are extremely torpid people. And in the not-too-distant past when broadcasters were getting into those bad habits, lazy old broadcast journalists had usually been lazy old newspaper hacks first. Ergo the lingering reliance on clapped-out standbys of the trade they'd left in the activity they founded.

All this boils down to one inescapable reality: if you can provide a statement to journalists that imitates as much as possible what they're used to seeing and doing – and hence is something they can rush into print or on to the air with as little thought or effort as possible – you're cookin' with gas.

In the print newsroom, the process of dealing swiftly with such public relations compositions is known as "typing '30' on the news release." The "30" is the traditional wire service way of indicating the end of a story. No one knows why, but the theories are all too boring and self serving to bear repeating here. Suffice it to say, even in this age of computerization, it's still widely used, possibly out of hidebound laziness. The expression (slightly adapted), "If you could get a communicable disease from a press release, that guy there'd be dead!" implies someone has taken a press release, typed "30" on the bottom and usually put their own byline on the top (more on this in a moment) and filed it as *their* own prose. While this often happens, more frequently journalists restore their virginity by rewriting (that is, slightly recasting) the first paragraph, and phoning up the contact name on the bottom of the release (more on this, too) and asking a couple of questions that have already been answered in the body of the text.

This way, a print reporter can write with a clear conscience a phrase like "Horace Schmoo said in an interview Thursday" after regurgitating a patently contrived quote from the news release. Making Mr. Schmoo sound like an articulate and thoughtful person, not the drooling lunatic that he in fact may be, is one big reason why public relations "counsel" are hired to cook up quotes for their countless press releases. The implication the story is the result of a thoughtfully conducted interview, in turn, conveys the impression to the reporter's supervisor that he or she is doing an exemplary job, actually talking with people and sometimes even wandering out of the office. Nothing of the sort may in fact be going on.

Speaking of exemplary work, bylines were noted a moment ago. Byline is the newspaper term for the line at the top of a news story that indicates it was written "by so-and-so, Staff Writer." In olden times, these did imply exemplary effort. As in, "didn't have to be re-written for five hours by some nameless copy editor," "actually makes some sense, for once," or, "remarkable, Watkins here has turned in a pretty good yarn!" Nowadays, unfortunately, bylines usually mean no such thing. Virtually every newspaper story gets a byline and noses get seriously out of joint when even a three-paragraph regurgitation of a press release doesn't. The likely culprit? Probably the invention of computerized data base services that insist it must be easy for users to search for stories by byline.*

Regardless, any reasonably intelligent person should be able to master the inverse pyramid style by reading their local paper for about five minutes. Even real dunces can figure it out, apparently. After all, of how many old wheezers, upon finally being wheeled out the door for the last time, has it not been said: "He was a really fine writer" in his youthful heyday? (However, all being able to write for a wire service will enable you to do is churn out a competent newspaper story, which, in fact, is the easy part.)

You Can Be Threatened with Power-Saws

Writing a good news release is a little more complicated, because it has to make you (or your political party, company or whatever) look good, or weasel you out of trouble. It also needs to do it in a way that doesn't seriously annoy, say, the senior vice-president in charge of another division. This is surprisingly easy to do. When you praise yourself or someone in your organization for doing a good job, it is axiomatic that someone else will take this as a veiled assault on the way they do theirs. I remember writing a press release for the B.C. Forest Service about what a great job one particular forest-fire-fighting crew was doing. Every other fire crew in the province took it as a mortal insult. If they had read it they were mad; if they'd only

---

*   Usually the user in question is the reporter who wrote the story in the first place, looking up painfully composed phrases from the "background" paragraphs to type into the latest version of the story.

heard about it, they were madder; if they'd only heard about it from someone who'd only heard about it, well, they were ready to come at me with the power-saw blades spinning! If you don't want to have this happen, keep the possibility in mind when you're writing the thing up and include a paragraph explaining that everyone else is doing simply fabulously too. Either that, or just say your industry's equivalent of: "Remember, folks, no smoking in the woods, and put out your blankety-blank campfires," and to heck with it!

So, first off, a good press release must convincingly mimic the wire-service style well enough that any spavined hack unfortunate enough to still be in the office when it rolls off the fax machine will figure it'd be a real shame to mess with it when he was about to head out for a beer anyway.

Second, it needs to be quite short, no more than two pages, double spaced, tops. You can write more than that if you want, but take my word for it, no one will ever read more. Journalistic attention spans being what they are, save your ink. Keep it tight, as they're forever saying in the trade, and it's much more likely to be used verbatim. That, after all, is the objective of this game.

Third, it must have a contact phone number (fax or e-mail are optional) at the bottom. The person named should be at the number if possible, or at least should be an actual existing human being, especially if you expect the release to be used by bigger, better staffed news organizations. This, however, is not absolutely essential. As a general rule, big news organizations will make at least a stab at checking the facts in a news release; small-town newspapers particularly can be depended upon to run them unchanged without the stab. One purpose of the contact name is to provide those reporters inclined to pick up the telephone someone to call to get a couple of quotes from. But even more important, since radio and TV reporters require tape with voices on it, they must talk to someone, in person or on the phone, who will repeat the information in the faxed handout they've just received. However, even if no one is in fact available, the contact name and number lends an air of verisimilitude, without which any reporter, no matter how lazy or stupid, may smell a rat.

Fourth, the release should begin with a one-line summary that suggests a positive headline, which, once implanted in an editor's head, will be almost impossible for him to shake. (Remarkably, even though they don't have to write headlines, this seems to work with broadcast-station lineup editors, too. This is probably because all their ideas that don't come from press releases come from that morning's newspaper.)

Now, if the news is good, you can just play it straight up in your release, as in:

> OTTAWA – 'Every man, woman and child in Placenta Narrows, Nfld., will be receiving a handsome cheque from the Government of Canada next week,' Luther Flootzwurtzer, Minister of Tents, Sheds and Awnings, said today. . . .

It's traditional, by the way, for public relations people to put in all those commas and capital letters so that the journalist who deals with the release can feel as if he or she is rendering the public a worthwhile and intelligently critical service by changing the phrase to read something like "tents minister Luther Flootzwurtzer."

If the news is bad, though, drafting an effective press release requires a more skilful hand.

Generally speaking, it is best to avoid outright untruths. This is especially true for publicly traded corporations, for which lies about certain matters, like financial results, are actually illegal and could result in jail terms for company officials. Better to sugar coat the bad news with an upbeat spin, and then bury the actual facts deep in the release. Extremely bad news of a sort that must be announced for legal or political reasons, such as the decision to cut a popular government program, for example, or catastrophic third-quarter financial results, should *always* be released late on a Friday afternoon, after the reporters who know what's going on have rushed off for the weekend. By the time Monday rolls around, and experienced reporters are again available, it'll be old news.

A Real Example

Here's an actual example of a news release, distributed by a large Canadian public institution late in 1993, that is an absolute classic of the genre, "LIBRARY BOARD INTRODUCES CHANGES TO BALANCE BUDGET" it summarizes hopefully.* It continues:

> With the aim of balancing a shrinking operating budget, the _____ Public Library Board today announced a number of changes to fees, hours and services which will go into effect Jan. 1.

This gets things off to a relatively breezy and cheerful start, as if someone in head office is doing a superlative job, without saying any of the bad things to come up high where a casual reader might notice them.

> Library Director [oh heck, let's change the names to protect the innocent] Leon Blotz explained that the decision to introduce these changes was made in anticipation of funding cuts from both the City and the Province.

Still no bad news, indeed no reason for it, but the blame for what's coming has been located squarely where it belongs, to wit, on someone else.

Blotz goes on to complain about the chintziness of the financing governments, then to note that:

> all the changes we are introducing are based on the results of surveys conducted over the past two years which indicated customers would opt for some service cuts and fee increases rather than face a tax hike.

This is clever, as we still haven't introduced the bad news, but we've blamed other people twice, said what's coming is your idea, not ours, and cited scientific-sounding research to back that

---

* See appendix I for the complete, actual news release.

assertion without telling us exactly what questions were asked. The questions may have been what is known in polling circles as a Russian ballot. As in, "Do you support modest user fees for poor people, or would you prefer your country to be run by vicious Communistic thugs who will beat up your family and take away all your stuff?"

Finally, in Paragraph Four, Blotz gets to the actual bad news:

> In the new year, the registration processing/ annual renewal fee for adults' and seniors library cards will go up by $1. . . .

And so, depressingly, on. You'll note that the annual charge for a library card, which is possibly illegal under the relevant legislation, is disguised as something else in a manner so arcane and convoluted that it's hard to comprehend what's in fact going on.

Wisely, the release concludes on a positive note, after repeating the plaint – through the medium of a manufactured-sounding quote – that the problem is really all someone else's fault. (I'm not making up a word of this, I swear, except the bit about Leon Blotz!) "This being the case," the release continues, "we will work more closely than ever with our customers to minimize the impact of those changes. . . ." As a final word, it promises more "initiatives" to reduce costs, not to mention a fund-raising campaign the following year.

And on an excellent note, it closes with " -30- " – a very professional touch – and, count 'em, *two* contact names, Blotz himself, and, "Marcia Maplethorpe, Manager, Communications." In fact, whomever your reporter calls, since the news is bad, it's Marcia she's going to end up talking to.

All in all, this is a masterful effort, worthy of study by aspiring politicians, corporate executives and members of the public service mandarinate: It packages bad news in an upbeat form, so that if it gets into print verbatim* it will leave readers with the reassuring impression all is well. It suggests a headline to

---

* It didn't.

reinforce that impression. Then it blames the bad news on someone else. It conveys the sense the institution's managers are working prudently to overcome everyone else's mistakes. It nevertheless fulfils a legal and moral obligation to outline the bad news, so that no one can complain later when they get the bill that they weren't informed. It fudges the institution's attempt to slide through a legal loophole to charge a fee it ought not to charge. It again points out the bad news is someone else's fault. But it implies the bad news is endorsed by the public – who in most circumstances will indeed be consulted, though not necessarily given any actual choices, about what horrible things should be done next. It promises all will be well in the future. And it does it all in a seamless, wire-service style that is extremely tempting to pick up and run unaltered. Adequate contacts are provided for radio and TV reporters to use for tape.

Given the laziness and ineptness endemic to many of the news media operations, the probability is extremely high that the message contained in a news release like this will pass into the public prints and airwaves like, ah, corn through a goose.

Photographic Immortality

Now, if you are sending out news releases, you may want to consider including a photograph or photographs. (But don't give them too much choice, they'll always pick the uglier of the two.)

This goes especially for the "media kits"* that you plan to send to newspapers and magazines, although television stations may also see some value in having your photograph on file, if you are still too insignificant to bother interviewing with actual moving pictures.

You should do this for a couple of reasons. For one thing, unless you look completely repugnant or have been seen by a number of witnesses committing a crime that carries a lengthy prison sentence, folks are probably more likely to vote for someone whose face they can visualize. This is probably why real-estate sales people have their photos printed on their business

---

*   Resplendent with news releases and bios as well.

cards and, presumably, why lawyers don't. Providing a photo gives a magazine or newspaper that might be disinclined to actually pay someone to snap your shot an opportunity to illustrate a story about you, and hence marginally increase your chances of election.

More important, though, having your photo on file can actually improve the "play" – i.e., the page and placement – that a newspaper story about you gets. This is especially likely to be true in daily newspapers, and it happens more often than you might think. The reason is simple: a lot of inside pages get slapped together with many insignificant stories on them, none of which have any available "art." The result can be pretty boring and the copy editors, or deskers as they are called, who design the pages know it. Now, some of them, at least, may be the sort who *want* to put out a better product if they can. So, if they *do* have a photo or illustration, they're tempted to display it more prominently than the story may in fact warrant – to wit, at the top of the page. As a result, a three-paragraph snoozer declaring your intention to run again for village council can suddenly be pumped up with irrelevant facts to justify its prominent placement on a weak page.

However, since the only person likely to be more unoriginal than the typical "photo journalist" – that is, someone who gets paid for going around taking hundreds of identical snapshots of the torsos and heads of middle-aged white males punctuated occasionally by shots of the remains of wrecked automobiles long after the last siren has faded away – is a typical photo journalist jumped up to editor, you will want to provide strictly conventional shots of your upper body and head. Anything more exciting and original will start to make a lot of people really nervous. Anyway, "original" shots tend to provide opportunities to make you look like a jerk later.

So the shots you choose should be taken in a manner that make you look as white and male as possible or, in the event you do not qualify for membership in either of those categories, strongly suggest that you possess such well-known white-male qualities as driving cars manufactured by General Motors, eating lots of starchy food, complaining about your spouse all the

time, playing golf and not understanding why *those guys* are
always whining about the cops, 'cause the police never give *you*
any trouble. ("What!!??" I can hear all you other white males
saying. Don't worry about it. It's a joke.) At the very least, try to
select a photo that imparts a little dignity, insofar as that is
possible.

For ease of mailing, the photos should be smallish, but for
convenience of use at the other end they shouldn't be too small.
About three inches by five inches is a nice size. Nowadays, by
the way, you should automatically include both a color and a
black-and-white shot, since as many publications require one as
require the other. And, for heaven's sake, hand them out like
business cards. Yeah, they cost a bit, but don't treat them like
they're $100 bills – it is a law of nature that no publication, no
matter what promises have been made to you, or how sincerely
they have been made, will ever return a photograph to you
undamaged. If your precious snapshot doesn't disappear completely, it'll come back bent, with strange grease-pencil marks
on one side and a sticker on the other containing esoteric, and
possibly quite insulting, printers' instructions. (i.e. "fat council
jerk, page Q76.") So why make people tell you lies?

At any rate, aside from the expense of having a suitable photo
taken and printed, there's little harm a standard "mug shot" can
do your election chances. Of course, smarter journalists may
keep the photo around in readiness for the day you are in deep
trouble and would do anything to keep your picture out of the
paper. But why worry about that? When that day comes, they'll
be able to get one from the cops or your opponents anyway.

Fending Off Alleged Misdeeds

Naturally, there are occasions when no news is the best news.
Just as corporations involved in shady practices seldom needlessly draw attention to those activities, it is axiomatic that
aspiring politicians should have the wit not alert the press and
public to questionable circumstances in their own pasts. Most
people understand this implicitly, and only issue statements
explaining away past misdeeds when forced to confront a leak
from the police or parole authorities, or a feature story in the
local daily outlining the irritating complaints of an intransigent

former spouse whining for a resumption of child-support payments.*

On the topic of simple denials, by the way, an offer to set the record straight in writing can lend an aura of credibility to your claims. As an excellent example, consider the day in May of 1991 when Mr. Ray Speaker, then a Conservative cabinet minister in Alberta, arose in response to an embarrassing revelation in the media and told the provincial legislature: "I want to make it very clear that the article that was written by Mr. David Climenhaga . . . has more than one inaccuracy, and it is my intent to address those by direct letter to that author."** No need to actually do as promised, of course. Certainly, as far as I know, Mr. Speaker – who now receives an even bigger public salary in Ottawa – never did.

However, should it be your misfortune to face serious questions about something really embarrassing, merely drafting an effective news release to defuse the situation will likely not be sufficient. Once the initial denials and spin doctoring have been completed and hurriedly faxed off to the eagerly awaiting hacks, measures are called for that in illiterate chamber-of-commerce argot are termed "proactive." (As opposed to reactive, presumably.) That is to say, the time has come to unleash an unremitting stream of cheerful news releases, each containing an entirely bogus but irresistible tidbit called a "news angle."

The theory behind this strategy is simple: Idle hands are the Devil's workshop.

Left to his or her own devices, the temptation to pursue an actual news story will occasionally overwhelm even an experienced journalist. This can be especially true if the reporter is a still-energetic rookie, or a sour old hack desperate for some final glorious fireworks. Thus the temptation to dig deeper into the news release, shrugging off, say, an aspiring politician's recently discovered bit part in a Canadian Airborne Regiment home video

---

* This is sarcasm, a well-known form of humor, so don't write a letter to the publisher about how hard your life is, thank you very much.

** *Alberta Hansard*, 2 May 1991, pg. 1034.

("some mistake, surely; must be my cousin from Saska-toon. . . . ") may prove as irresistible as an open and un-guarded bottle of Ole Snakebite to someone making his hungover way to a first AA meeting.

A stream of cheerful news releases, widely distributed, can rapidly cool such unwholesome ardor. Remember, most radio, television and print newsrooms are to some degree bureaucra-cies, hence dominated by bureaucrats. And media traditions being what they are, the best journalists and the worst news-room bureaucrats alike abhor being scooped, even when they know the scoop is worthless and they suspect they're being had. In the end, you see, it is far better for a reporter to put off doing a really great story that nobody knows about than to miss a piffling news release that, in the event, might attract the notice of a critic. So, if everyone in the business thinks everyone else has your latest trifling news release (say, because you happened to "accidentally" fax along your fax list), they will all be ex-tremely hesitant not to go through the motions before retyping it.

At this point, the inertia characteristic of so many journalists can be relied upon to take over. "Why work on another story when the day's already half gone? Anyway, the station line-up editor won't want two stories in one day about some dipstick who's only running for reeve of Remo Creek, right? What's more, I've filed a story and I feel like a beer. . . . " So the embarrassing mailing-list story gets relocated to the back burner. Another day, another press release. And another, and another, and an-other. . . . Eventually it's forgotten when something more sexy* pops up. And by that time, with a little luck, you've been elected.

One final note of caution: while it is essential to adopt a tone of high, if spurious, seriousness and authority in the composition of such documents, it is important to bear in mind who is supposed to be fooled by them. Ironically, sometimes the authors of these handouts, and the people for whom they work, fool

---

* As in, likely to get top play in the newscast, you know, *sexy*.

themselves! When this happens, they risk imperiously inform-
ing an inquiring reporter that "it's all in the news release" — as
if the statement were a quasi-official document, not subject to
questioning or revision. This is invariably a profound mistake.
Indeed, it is an excellent way to get a reporter to bother taking
the effort to put a negative spin on an otherwise well-crafted
news release. It is always wiser, when asked a difficult question,
simply to cheerfully answer another question of one's own composition.

5

Feeding and Watering the Media

How to avoid mismanaging conferences and thus avoid you and your organization becoming an international journalistic joke.

*L*et's be charitable. Let's call them "the Sproketarians." They're the service club from Hell. No working journalist has avoided an encounter with one of their nightmare luncheons.

Even in that fabled bygone era when reporters fought over lunch meeting assignments as payday drew close, no one in his or her right mind ever wanted to cover a Sproket lunch. (Even fewer do now that there's a minimum wage law in most provinces.) Really. People will actually choose to write about a search for a missing Great Dane or interview a bone marrow donor before going to lunch at a Sproket Club meeting. And it's not the boring and picayune speakers. Lots of clubs have boring and picayune speakers and newspaper editors don't have to threaten to break the arms of their reporters to get them to go.

Nope. The problem is that the Sproketarians, and their ilk, have been treating reporters like dirt since the invention of a free press, or at least since the beginning of Sprokets. And of course they're still at it, as shown by recent whining in the national media. The only difference being that when a national newspaper from Toronto snivels because a reporter got turfed from the part of a Sproket lunch where the PM is masticating, there's a letter of apology in the mail the next day from the prime minister's office. For the rest of us? Silence. And, you'll note, even for Toronto's most self-satisfied there was no apology from the Sproketarians.

Feed Me, Stanley, Feed Me

Listen, Sproketarians are terrible about feeding the media! Other clubs sit you with a bunch of hosers who complain the whole time about what's wrong with the media, which is annoying, especially since most of what they say is true and you know it. Others even sit you off at a table in the farthest corner and don't deliver your rubber chicken until the head table's finishing off those funny little pink whipped parfait things businessmen's club members always have for desert. (Why is that? What are they trying to tell us about their innermost selves by eating those fluffy, pink things?) This is, in everyday manners, rude, but at least a journalist has a pink parfait to look forward to.

But no! The Sproketarians – who imagine themselves the princes of the service-club set – sit you at a little, rickety table about two miles from the speaker, and *they don't even serve you lunch.* (Okay, sandwiches in the next room, for the *Globe* only, once.) That's right, if you're a normal reporter, you don't even get lunch. They won't even let you buy it!

You might get a coffee, if you're lucky – and if you're willing to put up with a linoleum salesman (tagged Sproketarian Merle or something) reminding you that "Youse guys from the media don't get lunch, only coffee." Unlike the coffee, when it eventually gets there, you're steaming. But then, consider the young woman beside you fresh out of the Moose Meadows Institute of Technology's commercial broadcasting course, she's just been told by Sproketarian Merle that "we don't usually let girls, er, (significant pause) ladies into our meetings." (And to think, they only allow one lino salesman per Sproket Club! Astounding!) Meanwhile, all around you, fat men in squeaky tight off-the-rack three-piecers from The Suit People and the really big aisle of Mr. Big 'n' Tall are borting down pounds and pounds and pounds (no metric for these guys) of cholesterol-packed pork and smacking their lips at the thought of their upcoming pink parfaits.

OK, I Have a Grudge

Man, it's enough to incite murder. Which is why generations of reporters and ex-reporters have been joyfully assassinating the characters of Sproketarians since before Granpaw was a freemason. (And I bet you thought it was because these clubs were peopled by overweight middle-class strivers who ringy-ding little bells with little hammers, tell a couple of mildly sexist jokes from the podium, bellow out The Queen in tuneless voices while a local member of royalty tinkles the ivories, and then address each other as Sproketarian Moe and Sproketarian Larry.)

Indeed, one of the most joyous moments of my own working career came the day the mayor of one of Canada's half dozen largest cities invited the city hall press gang, of which I was part, to hear his (predictably boring) annual speech to the Sproket Club. Apparently his aides and assistants didn't understand the way Sproketarians and reporters relate, and the invitation implied that lunch would be served. Of course, none of the media mob was fooled, having collectively been to thousands of Sproket lunches. So everyone ate enough to function, but not enough to take the edge off the general mean-spiritedness that makes it so much fun to carp and complain and make snide comments about Sproketarians Biff and Barry in voices loud enough to be overheard at the nearby tables where Barry and Biff had parked their ample behinds. But the coup was struck when we somehow persuaded one of the mayor's assistants, a polished young person with the potential for a better future, that, since His Worsh had invited us for lunch and the darn Sproketarians weren't going to cough up, she should send for takeout.

And you know, by gosh, she did! Right there in the hotel dining room, people in white jackets brought our stuff in and plopped it on the hitherto barren press table. And we got to snarl at late-arriving Sproketarians, who'd missed everything but the crusty pink parfaits and had the temerity to start eyeing our ribs and buns: "Hey! Get lost! That's for the *media*." It was a gleeful, happy, long-awaited moment.

The point of this tirade, er, *example*, is that Sproketarians as a class (which would be petty bourgeois, I guess) have never figured out how to feed and water the media. As a result, they've been chronicled for posterity as a bunch of witless hosers with less class even than Shriners – who, after all, not only build hospitals for children, but get drunk and fall off little tiny motorcycles, either of which are the kind of activities any reasonable person would appreciate (especially getting bombed and falling off a little motorcycle).

If you don't wish to be chronicled as a witless hoser, then you should treat the media in a courteous and professional manner – even if you actually think they're classless morons. (Of course, you could also call a news conference when it's not lunchtime.) That's it, truly all you need to know if you want the secret of effectively feeding and watering news reporters in hopes of effectively manipulating their reports. If you're running a fund raiser or a club meeting, give them the same arteriosclerotic lunch you're offering your other guests. If you happen to run across one of those journalistic puritans so naive or well off that he insists on paying for it, well heck, let him! If you don't know the price, just make one up and take the money. If he's only got Visa, and you don't take it, make him sign an IOU! Obviously the guy doesn't care because he's on an expense account. Bank on it, if he wasn't, he wouldn't be making the offer. And remember, for every effete hoity-toit from Toronto or Vancouver in a $60 bow tie who makes a big show of paying for everything, there're a thousand poor hacks in soup-stained polyester neckwear by Tip Top or Harry who'd kiss your pinkie ring just for a taste of the fluffy parfait, even if they get the one with the elastic top layer. Throw in a luke-warm coffee, and you could own them forever – or as long as none of their colleagues are looking, anyway.

Remember, reporters tend to be worse in groups, when self righteousness may break out at any moment – or, even more horrific, what passes for humor in journalistic circles. So it's always smarter to spread them around the room at tables occupied by people who don't talk when their mouths are full, rather than cram them all resentfully together at a distant "press table" where they could quickly go critical. You'll have the added bonus of actually doing a favor to those reporters who are serious about doing their jobs well.*

If you still feel contempt for reporters as a group, at lunch as elsewhere, just keep it to yourself. After all, just like the Sproketarians, you want free publicity – why else would you be inviting journalists to sip coffee while you break bread. (Granted, the fact that the Sproket boys keep getting it year after year proves you can ignore everything recorded herein, at least for now. But remember that you do so at the risk history – or the Toronto media, which is the next best thing – will put you down for posterity as a weenie!)

Let's Do Lunch

The same sort of rule applies if you yourself go out to lunch with a reporter. Always offer to buy and, if you can afford it,

---

*   Like me, for instance.

always offer to take her to a nice place. But if the journalist you're lunching with has a problem with that, don't push it. If she insists all she wants is coffee – really insists, that is – just let it go. Heck, you've probably been playing little jokes on Revenue Canada for years – just take yourself to lunch after your reporter has departed and put it down as a business expense. And if, God forfend!, you don't have an expense account – and maybe that's why you want to get into politics, eh? Well, make it clear you're just offering coffee because you know the press can only be bought on the newsstand. If you're lucky, your reporter may be dumb enough to take you seriously – or bright enough to take the hint and at least split the bill.

The same principle applies to news conferences, "photo ops" and other bogus "media events" – in other words, don't overdo it. You might embarrass someone. But for heaven's sake, provide coffee and sticky buns! I mean, these people have to eat and drink! Some of them may have forgotten to pack a lunch. It's practically a law of nature: sticky buns get results. Oh, and let your reporter buy *you* lunch now and then if he wants to. After all, he enjoys the thrill of exercising his meagre expense account, too. And why not? It's a business perk for everyone, right? Two lunches are better than one, etc. etc. So swallow your pride, and his lunch. It'll make him feel less guilty about the next five or six sumptuous repasts you set before him – but no less obligated!

It's *Not* Customary to Tip Your Reporter

Finally, there is the matter of giving gifts to reporters, which is common in some parts of the world but, alas, generally frowned upon in media circles in Canada. (I still remember the gorgeous Delft beer mug a famous Dutch brewer offered me, and which I turned down in a moment of ill-considered principle. I was on another continent, for heaven's sake! No one would have known. 'Aw,' I thought, 'I'll do the right thing and buy my own.' I rode a streetcar from the Hague to Delft that evening and priced one. A week's salary! Like Jesus, I wept.

In this country, as a general rule, the best advice is don't offer. Unless your reporter starts dropping hints, of course, in which case your choice is go along, as long as it doesn't cost too much, and always have something to use against him; or take the high road and pretend to misunderstand.

If you do offer some little thing – you know, like having one of your flunkies completely clean his car with a toothbrush, or a ride to Thailand on the government jet, back by midnight, no word to the missus – let him decline your offer as gracefully as he can, if he feels he must. As in so many things, we must learn that No means No. Likewise, if he insists on paying for something, let him. It's all in the name of keeping the media free of influence – so let him preserve his pathetic remnants of dignity by coughing up a few shekels for something you all know is worth a hell of a lot more. (In his heart of hearts, he knows you're giving him a deal, and he won't forget.)

If he just says No, you can always offer the same thing, "later," even if, as in the case of certain large auto makers' dealer-cost-plus-4-per-cent promises, you have no intention of actually delivering.*

So, let's review the correct way to feed and water the media: generously and thoroughly, but without embarrassing overindulgence. Beer will be fine; no need to offer take-home bottles of single-malt scotch unless someone starts dropping really heavy hints. Always quit while you're ahead – as the song goes, know when to fold. Don't push someone to accept something they don't want to. (They may just slam you to reclaim their virginity.) Always offer to pay. Gracefully let the other party pay now and again. Keep a mental note of everything.

Before you know it, you should have them eating out of your hand.

---

* Unlike some others, I am reliably informed, Ford Motor Co. of Canada Ltd. is as good as its word in such matters.

Advanced Media Manipulation

6

Leaking Confidentially

An uninterrupted stream of unmarked envelopes flowing from a politician to the media means a happy and productive relationship.

*N*othing keeps reporters happier than a steady stream of confidential documents.

Truly, nothing is more important to cementing a happy and lasting relationship between a politician and his adoring hacks than what are known in the news trade as "leaks" of confidential material. And just as, in the argot of journalism, waters are always shark infested, so do leaks always come in plain brown envelopes.*

Fortunately, there are lots of confidential documents that you can leak to the press at little or no risk to yourself. Indeed, the confidential documents you leak need not be certifiable secrets. You may, in fact, have sound reasons for keeping certain items out of the hands of the media, or even an occasional legal requirement to do so. Everybody understands this, even really dumb reporters. Heck, especially dumb reporters! (You can tell them *anything*, after all.)

Even if such a document should accidentally fall into the hands of the media, why panic? For starters, a significantly large number of reporters are too lazy or too overworked to actually work through a complicated document and, as a result, require your assistance understanding even the simplest documents, let alone those containing numbers. Indeed, they'd really prefer that you'd just give them a couple of swift, punchy quotes and save them the trouble of actually having to *read* anything!

This is unfortunate for the broad uninformed public, but lucky for you. It means that in most difficult situations caused by the accidental or ill-considered leak of something potentially explosive, the danger can be swiftly defused by appropriately timed mumbling, or a rush call to lunch with a developer (always a believable excuse at city hall, if not the school board). This all goes double for numbers. It is almost axiomatic that even the best journalists are in that business because they failed the math

---

* In reality, they're usually handed over the pristine table cloths of really interesting little Indian or Malaysian restaurants, accompanied by an entire bottle of delightfully chilled pouilly-fuisse. (For more details on feeding and watering the media turn back to Chapter 5.)

section of the Law School Admission Test. Glib though they may be, they cannot add and subtract, let alone multiply or calculate percentages.* (So it is interesting that in a news room with, say, even 40 or 50 reporters, a similar number of editors and a daily quota of "percentage" stories, there will seldom be more than one or two pocket calculators, and the guy who owns them both is always out. . . .)

In a real pinch, chances are you can get away with denying everything to everyone. Among journalists, the herd instinct is extremely powerful. (In real life, "scoops" almost never happen, and when they do, seldom anywhere but the best newspapers.)

So, if you've only leaked a document to just one reporter, reconsidered the wisdom of your act, and then start denying everything, chances are good he or she will quickly drop the story out of the intense fear that infects most media operations when they realize they're all on their own. As for your colleagues on town council or the schoolboard, they'll certainly believe you if you strenuously deny being the one to have made the unauthorized leak. After all, you can ask them, would a person of quality such as yourself fraternize with the media? Of course not! And anyway, you and your colleagues would certainly rather blame a hard-working, and preferably low-ranking, civil servant, whose livelihood can be threatened.

But let us pause here and digress for a moment. For while the constant leaking of confidential documentation is essential to your political health, nothing – absolutely nothing – is more pathetic than a politician who tries to leak his own correspondence to the press.

Alas, there is an office holder in every legislative body in every land who calls one or more of a none-too-exclusive group of reporters on a regular basis, usually late in the week when the poor hack is desperately busy cobbling together a long-postponed feature on potholes that the station manager has been demanding ever since his Grande Barge de Ville's super-hydraslush

---

*   A term has been coined to describe this situation: "innumeracy." The newsrooms of the nation, it goes without saying, are hotbeds of innumeracy, not to mention cliché.

suspension ("eliminates all annoying road feel") detected a slight irregularity in the roadway as he passed swiftly down from the part of town with a view through the part reporters live in. "Hi Dave," comes the dreaded voice over the telephone. "Better get over here right now! This is *really* big!" Right, sighs the hack. What, may I ask, is up? "Can't tell ya on the phone!" This said breathlessly, as if the phone lines were bugged. "I've already called [*fill in name of more energetic media competitor here*]! Better get over here RIGHT NOW!" The reporter groans and eases his bulk down the hall to the appropriate office, where a long wait ensues. (Sorry, chirps a flunkiette, His Nibs is now tied up on an important phone call. No doubt chatting with old Fill-in-name-of-competitor-here. The herd instinct being what it is, the hapless journalist, though sure the call is entirely bogus, dares not steal away.) Finally, he is admitted to the inner sanctum, only to be told: "Here's a copy of a letter I'm faxing to the chief commissioner this afternoon. I've really laid it on the line! Get rid of those clanky manhole covers or I'm holding you personally responsible, Chief, for the lost sleep of our fair city's blah blah blah blah blah. . . ."

Dear aspiring politician, please don't do this. As well as being pathetic, it is a risky strategy. Any reporter who knows anything about the office you hold – that is, the beat reporters you must deal with on a daily basis – will soon begin to ignore *everything* you say. They will also hold you in deep personal contempt, though this is less important, as it is probably inevitable anyway. You'll be forced to put up with the inconvenience of calling up lists of other reporters you know until you get somebody foolish enough, ignorant enough, lazy enough or desperate enough to publish what you want. This technique is outlined in more detail in the next chapter.

Threatening One Reporter With Another

However, one useful technique can be observed at work here. That is, the effectiveness – even with entirely pointless announcements – of manipulating the herd instinct of all journalists. If you really need something covered fast, don't hesitate to threaten one reporter with another. Chances are both will write what you want, even though they both know it's horsefeathers, just to avoid charges of having been scooped from bureaucratically minded colleagues and supervisors back at the home office. This even works with experienced, senior reporters who know what you are talking about. Do you doubt it? Just watch and compare today's big story from Ottawa on the various nightly news shows broadcast in your corner of the country.

Now, where were we? Oh yeah, necessary leaks. . . . Okay, despite the need to keep *some* things out of the hands of reporters, now and then every successful politician *must* leak an actual secret to a particular reporter or group of reporters just to keep the relationship with the media a happy and productive one.

Leaks: Not Just A Right, An Obligation

We're talking here about the real McCoy. The sort of document that makes civic chief commissioners just, uh, blanch when they think about who they're required by law to give them to — and who those people (i.e., you, if you manage to get elected) are sure to pass them on to (i.e., me). You know the kind of document we're talking about here: say, the board of commissioners' secret plan to bulldoze your town's central square, which dates back to the last Fenian raid, and replace it with a profitable car wash. The brass cannon will be kept for a nearby indoor mall in the post-modern-pastel-gypsum-drywall style prized by all Canadian urban planners. In other words: Civic progress! Job creation!

Leaking this kind of stuff pays big dividends. And this is why, for example, it's an open secret at every city hall and legislature in the democratic West, and no doubt elsewhere too, that there are always at least two politicians who can be depended upon to provide any desired document virtually on demand. Interestingly, a new source invariably sprouts quickly when an old one withers. This may also be why the media's sense of outraged betrayal and hurt is so palpable when an anticipated piece of confidential paper isn't for some reason coughed up in time to accommodate the pressure of deadlines.

Dividends

What dividends? Guess which politicians the media trot to for the formulaic and meaningless "reaction" the traditions of their profession demand every time one of the bogus "issues" that are the meat and spuds of Canadian politics at every level rears its unattractive noggin. (Now, that was a pretty ugly mess of mixed metaphors, sorry.) Well, in this day and age you can just forget it. In other words, leaked documents are the key to the free ink and air you crave. Quid pro quo.

Experts and Rent-A-Mouths

However, let us pause for a note of caution: Your objective in trying to be quoted frequently, at least as long as you are seeking election or re-election to public office, is to be perceived by the voting public as someone with credibility, someone who knows what he or she is talking about. (Not a genuine expert, of course. Such people exist, but they do not run for city council.) So you must beware the temptation to become what is known in the news trade as a "rent-a-mouth." It is not that rent-a-mouths are pathetic, they are not. It is just that this is not what you should desire to become at this early moment in your career. Reporters phone up experts or participants in a story when they need to understand something that is going on so that they can explain it to their readers or listeners. They phone up a rent-a-mouth when they *need a quote! Right now!* All too often, usually late in the day, a copy editor will feel the need to scratch the supervisory itch by demanding an additional "reaction" to the current non-event the reporter has had the misfortune to be writing about. And now and then, absolutely no one who actually knows anything useful is available to trot out the necessary quotes. This is where rent-a-mouths come in.

You see, rent-a-mouths will comment on *anything*, at any hour of night or day. And that is why all experienced reporters maintain a list of academics, cashiered labor leaders, failed book publishers, semi-employed "economic analysts," sometime free-trade negotiators, politicians forcibly ejected from office, retired chief executives, cashiered senior military officers, disgraced former ambassadors, ex-deputy ministers and many more who will say whatever is required whenever it's required. Indeed, some of these people can even be negotiated with, as in: "Say,

I'm writing a story about free trade with Blutovia and I need someone to say. . . ."

Now, being a rent-a-mouth is an honorable enough thing. It's just that you risk being used in a moment of need, rather than taken seriously and respected. And for now, *you* want to be taken seriously. The time to become a rent-a-mouth is after the voters have finally cottoned on to you and punted your butt out of office, and you need someone to talk to, buy you an expense-account lunch or just brown-nose you a bit for old times' sake. (Another reason, good any time of course, is if you are trying to launch an academic career.)

In the mean time, to return to the central advice of this chapter, you must remember that *every* successful politician, even those who are tight-lipped by nature, needs to – nay, *must* – provide confidential stuff to the media now and again. Else even promising careers may wither on the vine.

Those who don't tend this garden will see their press notices shrivel no matter how stunning and painstakingly staged are their official pronouncements, news events and "photo opportunities." More than one promising public career has dried up and blown away for this very reason. Fortunately, no green thumb is required in this patch of weeds. It is your good fortune as a Canadian public figure, no matter how minor, that virtually every word put on paper by a Canadian bureaucrat at any level of government, no matter how picayune or harmless, is nominally an official secret. That this tends to devalue genuine secrets has apparently occurred to no one. True, it also tends to obscure the odd real secret that does leak out, and maybe that's what the ubiquitous bureaucrats, who would obviously prefer to do all their business far from the prying eyes of irritating and meddlesome taxpayers, are thinking.

This Wouldn't Work South of the Border

As a result, there's plentiful material to leak. And since most of it is pretty harmless stuff, and virtually all of it is in the public's interest to know anyway, you can promiscuously pass it around to just about anyone with no feelings of guilt or conscience. It is always remarkable and mysterious, by the way, how much more open American public officials are than their Canadian counterparts. A lot of this stuff would never work in the States for the simple reason that the information is all officially public anyway, and because even the equivalents of deputy ministers answer their own phones and unblushingly tell the truth, even to foreign reporters.

But we're in Canada, thank goodness. So, naturally, the officials, administrators, bureaucrats and the like that you, the aspiring office holder, will soon have to deal with will try to make you *feel* guilty about even the possibility of leaking confidential documents. Pay them no heed. You and your long-term political success mean as much to them as your welfare and financial well-being mean to that guy in a plaid jacket who's trying to sell you a used Volkswagen. Less, probably. To them, you are like the old line about gals and streetcars.* A new batch of small-time politicians will be along in three or four years but bureaucrats go on forever; so why shed a tear for you, eh? They'll try to get you on side, get you to see it their way. And if that causes you to lose an election, well, so what? They've had their fun with you. Then they'll cast you aside like the proverbial used hanky.

So, ignore them!

This basic and rather unsavory bureaucratic urge to keep *everything* a big secret, especially when it pertains to how the public's money is spent, can be made to work for *you*. This is because the more documents that are officially secret, the more material you'll have available to win brownie points with reporters by wantonly passing around. Obviously, handing a reporter a completely anodyne public-briefing document is going to impress him or her less than discreetly passing over the same document stamped "CONFIDENTIAL."

To this end, you should quietly encourage your local bureaucracy's worst tendency by urging it to stamp Secret on as many pieces of paper as possible.

Consider the fine city of Calgary, my home, which is rapidly taking over from Regina the title of Athens of the Great Plains.

---

*   Or was that boys and streetcars?

Every page of almost every background briefing document prepared for that fine city's aldermen and officials comes with the big, beautiful, red, capitalized word CONFIDENTIAL stamped diagonally across it. Now, nearly everyone knows the true value of that stamp – to wit: virtually nil. Everyone also knows how the game is played, that is, you don't actually say where you got it, even though everyone can guess. Still, it gives even a well-informed reporter a little *frisson* of joy to be in possession of a document so marked. And it lets him begin almost every story with the words, "In a confidential document," thus falsely inflating – or, as it is described in the trade, "hyping" – the importance of the document, and hence improving the position, or play, of the story about it in the paper or on the newscast. I don't think readers and viewers are fooled by this. Nor are the editors who assign and supervise the stories. Certainly the reporters aren't. It's just that everyone feels the next guy in the chain must have been taken in, and so the game goes on.

So, I suggest that, immediately upon election, you get your town, village or city's bureaucrats to start playing the confidentiality game at once. The more things they stamp confidential, the better. Indeed, the more annoyed they are at you for leaking things, the better to let them know where they stand with the real world.

In fact, the problem you face as a politician is not whether to leak (of course you'll leak! Like the Titanic!), or even how much to leak (the more the merrier). Leak everything that doesn't make you look bad or hurt your own schemes, (someone else is bound to leak that). No, the problem is how to apportion exclusive scoops among the various competitive members of the press without hurting various other reporters' feelings.

Now, you may want to develop a special relationship with one or two reporters (See Chapter 7), in which case you'll probably leak more to that person than to others. Still, it pays to be reasonably catholic with your leakage, even if you're only a public school board trustee. Spread the joy around, even if you save the hottest stuff for someone you can work with. Keeps the natives from getting restless.

And remember, make sure that whoever gets that confidential document from you understands that you're doing them a big, big, really BIG favor, at great personal risk to yourself, only for the benefit of the taxpaying public, indeed of Mankind. Don't worry, everyone knows this is hooey, even those reporters who are not so smart. But everyone will love you for it, even the ones that are.

7

Friendships and Favoritism

Learn when to play favorites, when not to, and why having a pet reporter is essential.

Now we come to the delicate question of friendships and favoritism. That is, friendships with certain journalists, and favoritism that benefits those reporters over others.

Geneticism, Rewrites and Making Friends

Fortunately for journalism and the public interest, some politicians just love hanging around with journalists – for a while, anyway. But naturally, many do not wish to maintain actual friendships with journalists. Politicians find too many reporters ill-informed and unentertaining to talk to, or worse, inclined to drone on about their own affairs until all nearby eyes glaze over – and they are always on edge, fearing that some casual slip of the tongue may end up on the air or in the public prints. One suspects this may at least partly explain why journalists so often marry each other, often producing thoroughly objectionable offspring who are hired years later by their parents' friends and retainers. Thus, there may in fact be a genetic explanation of why the standards of North American journalism seem to be declining. Computers also play a role in this general degradation, especially in the realm of print journalism. The invention of the so-called laptop computer has permitted, even encouraged, untutored but nevertheless enthusiastic and confident graduates of Canada's many schools of journalism to file their meanderings whole cloth into newspaper computer systems. Once, such people would have had to file their inept accounts of current events to a tired old "rewrite man" – usually the victim of a recent alcohol-induced heart attack and hence no longer suitable for the exertion of reporting the news – which can involve walking and riding in taxicabs. "Rewrite"* would have done what his title implied, thereby producing a silk purse from a sow's ear. Now, alas, too much drivel often flows unvexed to the press.

However, this is no reason for aspiring politicos who do not enjoy the companionship of the press not to *feign* interest in, and friendship with, particular journalists. And it is *absolutely no*

---

*   As in, "Get me Sweetheart, Rewrite!"

reason not to favor those who are proven performers in the delivery of good headlines over those who may still retain tatters of objectivity or public service. Good heavens, no!

In fact, while standard public-relations-industry cant has it that one must be fair to all in the release of news, anyone involved in the essential publicity hounding of politics, or for that matter the journalistic hounding of politicians, knows this is errant bunk. Despite the "optics," as they like to say in political circles, the real motto of media-political relationships is "favor for favor," "scratch my back," etc. – and you'd darn well better not forget it! I mean, really, why would you deal with someone who didn't owe you a thing?

It is also true – particularly at the lowest levels of political and commercial life, precisely where those most in need of media-relations advice are likely to be found – that many, many stories are written, and hence broadcast or printed, solely because a single reporter has a personal interest of some sort in the subject matter. This can be as simple as a reporter who writes repeatedly about, say, trains because he or she likes riding on them. Or a journalist who keeps producing reports about a fundamentally uninteresting company or organization because he longs to see the receptionist with her clothes off.*

Now and then, there can be more complex motives, such as doing favors for a political fellow traveller or joining in a commercial conspiracy to defraud investors by touting a stock. Naturally, because many news organizations, like most large organizations, are bureaucratic by nature, once resources have been allocated to research and write a story, chances are minuscule that it will not be broadcast or published in some form. Moreover, once that has happened, chances are almost as small that some other hapless journalist will not be assigned to "follow" it, often repeatedly.

So, obviously, the key to successfully publicizing an otherwise boring political or commercial campaign can often be the interest

---

* Or his, this being the 1990s.

of a single reporter. Therefore, it is self-evident that any reporter who has such a personal interest in a cause that you are trying to pump should be identified and pandered to at once – though perhaps not to the degree you risk having your receptionist launch a sexual harassment suit.

Naturally, however, it pays to *appear* fair to all when it comes to the kind of pointless and boring "media events" that are normally laid on as a substitute for intelligent discourse between journalists and politicians nowadays. After all, media businesses are both competitive and, as has been noted, often bureaucratic. Thus, if one is not to make dangerous enemies, it is best for all known reporters to be informed of the time and location of the bogus staged events that are the staples of journalism in places like Ottawa and the provincial capitals. That way, no one has to explain to his or her chief office bureaucrat how they missed the news conference everyone else managed to find. The wisest response to an accidental omission that gets someone in trouble, is to immediately send a flunky, if one is available, to engage in some really degrading grovelling. By no means, however, should you do this yourself. Everyone understands that all must be told of the hour and location of the next tightly controlled photo op, and no one is offended at the lack of exclusivity. Indeed, why would a reporter want to go to a press conference alone, unless it was to have all the sticky buns to himself? I mean, standing around with other reporters carping about what swine the politicians are, in precisely such terms, and worse, is half the point of such affairs, is it not?

Maintaining Your Pet Reporter

Nevertheless, it is absolutely axiomatic that all sensible politicians cultivate and favor particular journalistic pets. And politics is not like marriage (southern Utah excepted): you can have more than one, without guilt. The reason you pick a particular reporter may be because you are ideological fellow travellers, because you actually like and admire one another (unlikely as this may seem to you if you've just been the subject of an embarrassing media attack), or because of the basest of back-scratching considerations. Remember only this: if you must choose between a pet you sincerely admire and one that you don't who can effectively help your cause, you should obviously select the latter.

One maintains such relationships through all the usual gestures that are dealt with elsewhere in this manual: leaking confidential documents is of course the foundation of most long-lasting unions. So too are friendly "business lunches" (most, but not all, of which are on your tab), and being uncomplaining and available at inconvenient hours to provide desperately needed quotes. (Reasonable rules of engagement can be worked out to ensure your pet never calls, for example, your special friend's secret apartment or your family's children's telephone line, except in the direst of emergencies.) You may also consider comradely offers of professional sports tickets that your previous employer the development company would have thrown out anyway (tee hee), or possible employment for a spouse or child. Even morale-boosting late-evening "consultative" phone calls to journalists at home are useful. However, it is important to note that this should be done only if you rise to the rank of mayor, minister of the Crown or above. A reporter no more wants to hear from a mere alderman or school trustee after 5:30 p.m. than you want a drunken journalist telling dirty jokes about sailors and orangutans at your youngest daughter's garden party.*

But remember, since the day will come when an emergency forces you to ask a journalist to deliver unto you a service that is really quite unsavory, even to a reporter for a chain of tabloid newspapers, it is worth making a mental note of all gifts, favors and benefits you have delivered to your pets. (Remember how the famed Soviet KGB drew victims into its sinister web. First a round of dinners and friendly drinks; then perhaps a tour of a place and building, or a visit with a bigwig, denied to others; then a completely legitimate little business project, say, a freelance article for *Pravda*, a short research note. Entirely legitimate, paid handsomely, receipt provided. One is always asked to sign the receipt, of course. Another little project, another receipt; another and another. . . . Do not, repeat, do not, however, take

---

* The only one I know also involves a bartender and a hammer.

this advice to mean you should try to get reporters to sign chits for favors. This is a metaphor. Journalists will grow surly and suspicious if you follow this advice too closely.

The reasons for all this are obvious – and less than obvious. You are, after all, by profession and inclination a publicity hound – why else would you be seeking to gain or retain public office. And it is obviously beneficial to you to have a professional relationship with someone who can uncritically publish your self-serving blatherings in a place where members of the unsuspecting public can be tricked into reading them as if they should be taken seriously. This is the basic quid pro quo for all those lunches and confidential documents. The journalist also gets something out of the relationship – to wit, bylines, the only known measure of journalistic productivity, personnel-department claims and journalism trade-review articles notwithstanding. (If you are a novice politician, and you should somehow manage to get elected, your pet reporter, quite naturally, will want you to believe that your good fortune all happened because of him or her. This is worth about what it seems, but swallow your mirth and act as if it's true. Trust me, things will work out more happily this way.)

It is important that someone think of you when a routine "reaction" comment is required. Having a pet means someone always will; ergo, more publicity. Likewise, a tame journalist of your own provides you with regular opportunities to plant self-serving rumors. Your journalistic favorites can then help you immeasurably by asking your political opponents about these fictions, then printing their guilty-sounding denials.

But the most valuable services such favorites can render take place during moments of real crisis. Should you be so stupid or unlucky as to really find yourself up the creek without the proverbial paddle, that is the time to call in those long unforgotten favors.

"Sports Reporters Defamed as Class"

Let me give you an actual example: Some years ago, a colleague of mine who covered local politics for a small radio station in Central Canada became aware of an attempt by a minor-league professional sports team to blackmail the town council into building a new arena at the taxpayers' expense. This is an absolutely routine part of the professional sports business, and municipal councils seldom fail to immediately fold and hand over all the money. Two or three seasons later, the team leaves in the dark of night for a new town, where the process begins anew. The blackmail scheme hung on new operating subsidies mandated by the league, and a time limit after which, well, a new home city would just have to be found.

At every turn, my friend's attempts to report on the scam were blocked or countered by the station's sports reporter, who treated each team press release like a swing of a grim pendulum. (It is a law of nature that broadcast sports reporters will do anything the teams they cover tell them to, even if it involves violating the laws of God and Man, or even the unwritten code of prison inmates! It is the principal reason sports coverage, aside from the games themselves, is so unrelentingly boring. Amazingly, though, not one is known to have contracted a fatal immune deficiency from the industry's routine techniques for handling sports teams' press releases.)

Anyway, one slow afternoon, my colleague hit upon the notion of telephoning the league president in a far-off U.S. Sunbelt city. This grim personage was perpetually unavailable, according to the sports reporter, who insisted that it was necessary to submit written questions and await faxed responses at the league's convenience. Within about 15 seconds she had the fellow on the line. He was soon prattling cheerfully into her tape recorder about professional sports, fishing on the sparkling blue waters of the Gulf of Mexico, which could be seen from his office window, and, of course, the league's subsidy requirements. "Oh, those," he chuckled. "Don't mean a thing. We've dropped all that junk 'til at least next year. . . . "

Alas, the foolish girl put in the standard "reaction" call to the local team. When, as anticipated, its executives failed to call back, she joyfully recorded her item and went home naively confident she had struck a blow for fiscal responsibility in municipal affairs. That evening, though, she found herself at home staring bug-eyed as her radio blathered. A "late-breaking" account by the sports reporter recounted how, shortly before deadline, the team had announced it was generously allowing the city a year's extension on the requirement for increased taxpayer subsidies!

What had happened, she came to suspect, was standard damage-control employment of the nearest available pet reporter. When the penny dropped with team management that someone was on to their scam, a panicky call went out to their favored local spear-carrier. Markers were called in, slightly unsavory benefits remembered, and a more acceptable report substituted. (The team subsequently departed for Toledo, Tulsa, Topeka or some such place, taking the taxpayers' pucks with it.)

I myself experienced a similar event, at once more egregious and less shocking, when working for a famous Toronto-based financial newspaper. Ordered to follow up on the financial difficulties facing a well-known retailing company, I called the firm's head office in another city. For a time I bounced from representative to representative, repeating my probing questions – i.e. "Where did all the money go? Are you broke? Will your board of directors have to go to jail?" – and getting no answers.

Finally I was asked to await someone who was authorized to tell all. An interminable passage of time followed. I viewed this as nothing extraordinary, as journalists spend half their lives nowadays listening to elevator music on telephonic hold. Eventually, though, someone tapped me on the shoulder: My pursuit of the story was no longer required. I set the telephone aside, puzzled.

It developed that, while I waited, the company had analyzed their predicament, drafted a swift, self-justifying statement, and telephoned another employee of the same newspaper who for one reason or another was more sympathetic to their self-inflicted plight. He quickly took it all down verbatim and filed it as his own while I waited on the line.

At the time, put out by the inconvenience, I was outraged and vowed revenge. Over the years, however, I have come to appreciate both the sheer brass of this response and the skilful use of a pet journalist. If you are serious about a career in politics, you should ponder this story carefully.

You're Not Going Steady

Having said all of the preceding, however, we must pause briefly to remind ourselves that our relationships with favored pets are not something sacred, like your pledge to the Elk's Lodge. On the contrary, unlike going steady, you are entirely within your rights as a politician, should you not be able to get immediate satisfaction one place, to try somewhere else at once.

Indeed, if your pet relationship is with a "beat" reporter – that is, a journalist assigned to cover your particular level of government on a fairly regular basis – he or she is likely to have a pretty good idea that you're full of baloney when you come tripping down the hall with whatever self-serving line of bunk you're peddling to get your name in a headline. That's the problem with people who know what you're talking about, or even who simply have reason to suspect that you don't. But be of good cheer! A rejection by your usual pet in such circumstances is absolutely *no* reason to stop using that particular line of hooey in your clamor for ink. *Au contraire!* Immediately try another – and another, and another, and another, if necessary – until you find someone willing to give good headlines. The search should not take you too long.

Consider, for example, the story of the village councillor in a community near you who subscribed to the foolish notion that provincial lottery revenues go into a huge slush fund, for which there is no accounting, for the exclusive use of members of the governing party in each province. This modern Canadian myth is substantially without merit, yet widely held by ignoramuses. The facts of the matter, should you be such an ignoramus – which is a distinct possibility if you're considering a big push to become a village alderman – are that lottery revenues in every Canadian province are at least properly and publicly accounted for; and mostly disbursed to such worthy causes as expensive medical equipment and capital-intensive sports facilities. That these are invariably located in the ridings of members of the governing party is another matter. The point is that they aren't simply poured, holus bolus, from an enormous slush fund.

So when the school councillor phoned her pet weekly newspaper reporter and breathlessly demanded the government start accounting for lottery funds and, what's more, using them at once to finance education, he hesitated. Foolishly, he checked and was speedily set straight by the nearest lottery corporation. His mistake: failing to immediately and carefully inform his supervisor that the "news tip" had been checked and was total horse pucky. Indeed, he loyally called back to warn the politician not to say something so foolish in public, painstakingly outlining the actual true facts. So imagine that reporter's astonishment when he read the following week's edition of his own paper and came across the identical attack, complete with the identical politician assailing the government's fictitious lottery slush fund!

The councillor, sensibly enough, merely needed to keep hitting on reporters until she found one ignorant or lazy enough to parrot her line. Hers being a small town, that process required only one additional call. She likely knew her loud complaints were unsupported by facts. That hardly matters in politics, as the reporter who deprived himself of a well-placed story should have known. The trustee's rant was soon picked up and disseminated by regional broadcasters and newspapers, all of whom relied on each other, not the brains God gave them, for their daily news judgment. No one cared that her claim was bereft of merit. Not even the accused government, which was too canny to deny her assertions, promising instead to investigate the matter thoroughly and roll some unwanted civil service heads.

Selecting Your Reporter by Numerology

One other consideration may be relevant to the selection of a personal journalistic pet. That is, the longevity and productivity of the patron-pet relationship. Naturally, one wants any business dealings upon which tax-deductible entertainment expenses are lavished to bear as much fruit as possible. But you are likely to be operating at the most insignificant levels of politics possible. And you will probably remain there. Nevertheless, school trustees have been known to become prime minister of Canada, if not for very long, so anything's possible. Because your political prospects are so insignificant, it is also probable that you will be dealing with the most insignificant political reporters available. (Which is to say, near the bottom of the journalistic heap, but not quite at it.) So determining which of several possible pets will go farther than the others – and hence help your career more, for longer – may present difficulties. There are no sure-fire guarantees. As a general rule, though, we do know this: a young woman will typically go farther in the news media nowadays than a young man with an ordinary sounding name. However, a young man with two last names will go farther than any young woman. So, put your money on the fellow with two last names. (In the unlikely event you are forced to choose between *two* fellows with two last names each, bet on the one with two *first* names for last names. As in Peter Stevens beats Wilson Rawlings beats Mary Smith beats Dave Katzenjammer.)

One final note, though an is extremely important one, is that sometimes, among people of particularly bad judgment, politicians' relationships with their pet reporters progress beyond petting. In the unlikely event this should happen to you, or to someone upon whom your career depends, extreme care must be taken. This is for the sake of your pet's career and, much more important, your own. In such a case, the single vital rule that must be remembered at all times is this: do not – repeat, do not – make arrangements for liaisons, wine purchases or the type and color of pyjamas to bring, over a cellular telephone. Repeat: *cellular telephone calls are not secure*, especially if your special friend works for a radio station. Almost anything else can be persuasively lied about. But a trail of credit card receipts entered into court as evidence, or a convincing sounding transcript or tape-recording of a cellular telephone call broadcast by a talk-radio station will sink you every time.

8

Holy Writs and Damning Prose

Should you sue for defamation? What you can gain, what you can lose.

"Clearly, Ald. X is a homo sapiens and a bibliophile, and no more need be said!"

Novice politicians often ask: "Should I sue?" What a silly question! *Of course* you should sue!

Suing journalists for libel is one of the most effective, if least understood, weapons in your media-manipulation arsenal.

Thanks to Canada's libel laws, politicians can not only silence critics and suppress inconvenient criticism, they can often effectively manipulate the media into handling news events in a manner more helpful to advancing their own political careers. Moreover, if they possess a really shrewd understanding of these laws, they can achieve positive results with a minimum of expense.

Yet many novice politicians blunder badly, not to mention spend far too much money, when they try to use defamation laws simply to protect their damaged reputations.

Remember, once you have decided to run for a public office, especially an insignificant one, your reputation is already damaged beyond repair. Your aim should not be to try to repair damage, or even to exact revenge (although that can be highly satisfying) but *to achieve your political objectives.*

Confusion over the proper reasons for suing journalists for libel likely springs from a common misconception. To wit: that Canada's defamation laws exist for the protection of people's valuable reputations. In reality, of course, nothing could be further from the truth.

But don't feel foolish because you have fallen for this old legal wheeze and never gotten up – your confusion has fairly normal underpinnings. For starters, the first time *you* think of suing someone for libel will probably be on an occasion when your reputation is indeed under attack, quite possibly unfairly. And even if the attack is entirely justified, especially if it may result in your spouse suing *you* for divorce, it will sting all the more. Furthermore, the powerful Canadians who drop libel writs like snowflakes in winter (and their high-paid legal help) never tire of perpetuating the myth it's reputations they're protecting.

Such nonsense, repeated ad nauseam, can be persuasive, at least to folks who aren't paying attention.

Suppressing Free Speech

The truth, of course, is that the principal purpose of Canada's defamation laws is to suppress criticism of powerful people and institutions. These laws today exist, quite obviously, almost exclusively to curtail legitimate free speech.

Not so obvious, you say? Consider this: if the real purpose of defamation law was to protect valuable personal reputations, then ordinary taxpaying citizens (whose reputations can actually affect their ability to make a living) would have practical access to some legal means of protecting their good names.

Of course, nothing could be further from the truth. The reality is that *actually going to court* and suing somebody for libel is pretty much a rich man's game. But since in Canada – quite unlike the United States, where free speech is taken seriously – the cards are so heavily stacked in your favor once you can afford to ante up the game's entry fee, it pays the rich and powerful to play.

This is because once a journalist or author – or even a humble writer of letters to the editor – has been served with a writ of libel, he is likely to soon discover what it was like to be hauled before the notorious Court of Star Chamber. This is literally true, by the way, for that is the very place, during the reign of the first Queen Elizabeth, where the modern tort of libel, as used so effectively to muzzle legitimate speech in Canada, took on its present form.*

---

* The Star Chamber's judges, perhaps with some justice (no pun intended), would have excused their suppression of printed free speech as necessary to maintain social order in a fragile society beset by a revolutionary new form of communication. (Much as loony feminist college professors nowadays argue that the Internet must be muzzled to make the world safe from masturbatory adolescent fantasies.) No such threat to social order can be imagined today from reporters who would dare to discuss, say, the financial history of certain captains of industry. If reputation was truly at issue, a more sensible tort for protecting reputations than Star Chamber libel proceedings would be the Common Law on slander (that is, spoken, unrecorded, defamation). The (continued on the following page)

Guilty Until Proven Innocent

While Canadians accused of criminal offenses may be innocent until proven guilty, when it comes to defamation they are
guilty – oh, pardon me, my learned friends, "liable" – until they
prove themselves innocent. (Which they frequently can't, so
stacked are the esoteric rules of this tort against the accused,
whoops, the defendant.) Moreover, the financial penalty for
writing an unprovable truth about a powerful fellow-citizen, or
even just crossly voicing a completely justified grievance in print
or on tape, can be far more severe than that for, say, killing a
child with an automobile while extremely drunk or severely
beating up your spouse.

Of course, theoretically, you have a right to make a "fair
comment" on the issues of the day. But, while this is not the place
for a long discussion of the arcana of defamation law, it is
important to note that the "fair-comment defence" must be based
on facts. And not just any facts will do – only those that you can
prove in a court of law. In other words, to take an example from
a news story of the moment, you're *allowed* to comment that a
particular fellow ought not to have murdered his wife. But – in
Canada, at any rate – you'd darn well better be able to prove that
he *did* kill the poor lady.

Speaking of financial penalties, one other motive suggests
itself for suing people for libel: Huge damage awards. But who's
ever heard of anyone – excepting lawyers, of course – really
getting paid these big damages? It may happen, but if it's
sure-thing cash from a court settlement you want, get someone
to crash into your car or knock you off your bicycle. At least their
insurer will have a pool of funds to pay you from.

So an aspiring politician on a tight budget must understand
the simple realities of Canadian defamation law before he or she
can devise cost-effective strategies to use accusations of libel for

former requires no proof that actual harm has come from the statements complained
of, the latter does. No special legal knowledge is required to guess why libel, not
slander, forms the basis of most Canadian provinces' defamation acts.

what they are truly intended – suppressing criticism or, better yet, effectively manipulating the media.

Just for starters, consider as a model of the effectiveness of this law (a blunt instrument for suppressing legitimate free speech) the case of the late Igor Gouzenko, who sued almost everyone using money that you, the ever-generous Canadian taxpayer, kindly provided for almost everything. It worked out great for Igor!

Remember him? He was the Russian cypher clerk who went around appearing with a bag over his head for years after he'd absconded from the Soviet Embassy in 1945 with the pile of secret spy papers that essentially started the Cold War. (The bag bit is interesting, since the KGB and the NKVD and their ilk obviously knew what he looked like. Maybe he was worried about what Canadian taxpayers would think if they found out what he was using all their money for.)

On Defection Day, Igor started by going to an Ottawa newspaper, where a pitiable night copy editor told him to take a hike and tell the cops about it – and then lived the rest of his career in professional ignominy. (Even the poor guy's obit went something like: "Joe Dipstick, the pathetic fool who. . .") Which may account for why Canadian journalists – every one of whom has sent an obvious lunatic packing at least once in his or her career* – always sort of wondered if there wasn't something more, or less, to Igor than met the Cold-War-conditioned eye. Come to think of it, it may also explain something about Igor's later combative relationship with the press.

One reporter even wrote a novel – long after the man was finally dead, of course – suggesting that he was put up to defecting by his masters in the KGB so that he could spend years fingering perfectly loyal Western public servants as Soviet "moles." Far fetched? Who really cares? The point is that, as long as he lived, no one in Canada ever said or wrote *anything* bad

---

* In my case it was a guy who figured that cops-on-the-take were helping armored-car robbers dressed up like armored-car guards rob armored cars, and, oh, by the way, has Jesus come into your heart. . . . You get the general idea.

about Igor because he sued *everyone* who had the temerity to whisper, let alone write, a faintly critical word about him.

Libel Chill – Publicity Chill

Talk about "libel chill!" Dealing with Igor – for years a resident of the Toronto suburb or Mississauga, which come to think of it must have made him feel at home after Russia in the 1930s – became such a pain in the behind for Canadian news executives that the journalists they employed almost completely stopped writing about him.

Of course, thanks to the proud Common Law tradition that you can't defame the dead (or at any rate be forced to pay damages for doing it) journalists started getting their own back before Igor was cold. Similarly, reporters today remain mostly silent on the more loathsome activities of several prominent people rich enough to sue anyone who spells their name correctly, and who aren't mentioned here for that very reason. However, don't conclude that my defamation of business people as a group – fortunately not something one can yet be successfully sued for despite the recent efforts of certain Royal Canadian Air Force veterans – means this is just some sort of rich capitalist thing. *Au contraire*! The college-educated and politically correct Canadian left seems to endeavor to suppress opinions that they disagree with – whoops – protect their reputations, with a vigor and enthusiasm unsurpassed by all but a few Canadian plutocrats. (Only in British Columbia, though, have this crowd, with their so-called human rights legislation, actually attempted to outlaw free speech throughout an entire province.)

If anything, in fact, the wingy Left is better at this kind of thing than the Old Right, which at least had the dignity to admit they were suing to shut the opposition up, and not to cook up politically correct doubletalk about how you have to destroy free speech to preserve it.

However, getting back to Igor, the point is that his was an exercise in pure Stalinist thuggishness – designed only to silence all critics, real and imagined.

If, unlike Gouzenko, you are a would-be Canadian politician aspiring to insignificant office, you have other things to think about. If your big ambition is to become the mayor of Yahk, B.C. (or for that matter, Yak, B.C.) or Mushaboom, N.S., not only can you not financially afford to sue everyone who offends you, *you don't want to*! Unlike Igor Gouzenko, you *crave* free publicity. Desperately. Let's say that again: YOU'RE DESPERATE FOR FREE PUBLICITY! So you can hardly afford to poison the well so that no one dares put your name in the local community weekly or utter it on the AM Country & Western station's news broadcast, can you?

Anyway, why should you even be thinking about suing people for bad coverage when really good coverage is so pathetically easy to get? In most places in Canada, you've got to be really inept, or incredibly unlucky, to get mildly criticized in the media, let alone slammed.

The Five Dumbest Words

In fact, most novice politicians intuitively know this, even if they don't consciously recognize that they know it. It's just that they get so darned mad at some two-bit local columnist or smart-mouthed disc jockey that they can't restrain themselves from uttering the dumbest five (four?) words in Canadian politics. To wit: "I'll sue you, you bastard!"

Stupid politicians and stupider would-be politicians are *always* threatening to sue reporters for journalistic slights, real or imagined – inevitably calling their legitimacy into question as part of the deal. Now, even if you had the funds to sue for defamation, and *despite* the way the courts stack the deck in favor of litigators, there are nevertheless times when an aspiring politician, especially an unelected one, just can't win. If you are new to the game of politics, and you have just ejaculated these words, or ones like them, chances are that this is one of them.

Nine times out of ten, if you don't have a legal leg to stand on, the reporter you're mad at will know it. And, sometimes, when you *do* have sound legal grounds, a reporter may believe you don't. And because reporters hate and fear *real* libel suits, they're likely to go into a feeding frenzy when they suspect they're being frivolously or ignorantly threatened by someone they can get away with putting a blade into. Others may join in for the pure joy of it.

The result, even if you have a good case in law, may be that you *lose the election*. And what profiteth a man to gain the whole world if he loseth the vote?

The journalistic motto in such circumstances is "No reason to stop kicking a man just because he's down." If seriously annoyed reporters sense you can't afford to sue — and think about it, you probably can't — they'll start kicking. Hard. (By the way, no one has a thinner skin than a journalist. As a class, they can always dish it out, but they can hardly ever take it. So if *you* ever say anything mildly unkind in print or on the air about a specific one of *them*, guess what five words *you're* going to be hearing next.)

The point is, never! — Never! *Never!* — tell a reporter you're going to sue. Bite your tongue. Just don't say it.

Which is *not* to say you should never sue. Absolutely not. Remember, once you've actually started suing, the libel laws of this country work for you. But if you decide to actually sue, pick your spots. Consider carefully such factors as the state of your finances, the strength of the legal team arrayed against you, the potential harmful effect on the free publicity you crave, and the likelihood of winning enough to not have to bother pursuing a career in politics. (Some lawyers are capable of advising you about this sort of thing. If yours advises, "Drop it!," he's probably being honest.)

No Need To Actually Sue!

As we shall observe in a moment, it may not be necessary to actually risk the expense of going to court to derive many of the benefits of a good lawsuit. But if you *are* going to sue, sue already! If you're just bluffing, you should also have your lawyer get on with drafting a threatening letter. Either way, though, don't go telling everyone about it before you actually do anything. Think of the egg on your face when your "watertight" case starts springing leaks like a colander, or you chicken out when you discover what your lawyer charges to write a threatening letter — or, maybe worse, you agree to pay his exorbitant rates because you're too proud to be chicken.

Just quietly let your legal counsel drop your writ and get your pleasure from imagining the poor schmuck's face as the dreaded piece of paper lands, whack!, on his desktop. Or quietly forget it and don't risk embarrassing yourself.

Remember, nothing here says you shouldn't actually sue someone for libel, just that you shouldn't sue unless it helps you achieve your political objectives. Which probably means, as tough as this may be at times to swallow, that you should never sue anyone if you're just one of 25 or 30 complete unknowns lining up for an insignificant civic by-election somewhere.

Once you're elected however – and have some income – there may be good reasons to actually sue people for defamation. And there certainly may be strong reasons to appear as if you might sue them.

This is a very important point: A good writ, even though you have no intention of actually following up on it, can be just as effective and satisfying as an actual lawsuit. More so, actually, because after the initial thrill, a real lawsuit soon becomes protracted drudgery. Moreover, a threat for threat's sake won't leave you in financial ruins as the benefactor of yet another happy lawyer.

Silencing Troublesome Journalists

You can use actual legal action, or just a convincing threat that you have no intention of following up on, to discipline, or if necessary silence, troublesome local journalists. If you do this, though, you'll want to drop writs sparingly to avoid "publicity chill" – which is just as deadly to aspiring politicians as "libel chill" is to a free press. And you'll need to make special efforts to keep other journalists on side. (Refer back to Chapter 5 for more information on personal relationships with reporters.) Remember:

> *Dave's rule number 500* – a properly thought out and well-directed writ can silence, or at least muffle, even major newspapers and broadcast organizations.

The trick here is never to take on large media corporations directly unless you have either an absolutely airtight case or an unlimited supply of cash. They pay top lawyers to squash guys like you like bugs, and their pockets are almost certainly deeper than yours. (If they're not, why are the guys who own them living in Chief Executive Heights while you're running for dogcatcher from the wrong end of Railway Avenue? Eh?)

Fortunately for you, taking aim at a smaller and more vulnerable target – say a community weekly or a university student newspaper – can more effectively silence the big players than taking them on directly. Ironically, if you fight the big guys they'll use their lawyers to fight you right back. But smaller players don't have the money they'd need to test your questionable case in court. So they'll bluster for a couple of weeks, then back off and print the grovelling apology you demand.

But word gets around pretty quickly in journalistic circles. And mid-level managers at big media operations whose reporters get into lawsuit trouble often find themselves in managerial hot water. So, thanks to a couple of well-placed threatening letters, before you know it, you can gain a reputation as someone who wins libel suits. (Even though you have done no such thing and, indeed, have never been inside a courtroom except perhaps as the defendant in a criminal case.) Then, there's a good chance that a timid, desk-bound decision-maker at big broadcast station or newspaper will make his reporters back off too, or at least handle your pronouncements with kid gloves. *Et voila!* You've successfully chilled negative reporting about you.

But beware, in addition to the risk of chilling publicity, using writs or actual suits this way increases the danger someone might really go after you when they finally have something solid. (Here too, though, you can come out ahead, because once you're known as an effective litigator – even though you're no such thing – institutional timidity and laziness will often make it extremely unlikely that anyone will bother to make the effort to get the goods.)

Astound Your Friends

But should the unthinkable happen, my counsel to you is to take the advice of Mark Twain and tell the truth, "You'll astound your friends," he said, "and confound your enemies." What the heck, if you let *all* the bad news go in one blast, there'll be one or two terrifically bad big stories, and then everyone will forget about it. Let it drip out one putrid drop at a time and heaven knows where things may end up. If Richard Nixon had understood this elementary truth, he'd probably have finished his term and someone like Dan Quayle would be president of the United States today!

Then again, you could do like the physician in the States who squelched – or at least suppressed – the rumor he has AIDS by offering a $2,000 reward for any information that would allow him to successfully sue the originator of the damaging story. Apparently it had the desired effect and shut everyone up. (No word on the doctor's health, though.) Of course, if you try this, there's always the danger you'll have to pay *and* sue.

Dead and Libelled

Speaking of which, regardless of the condition of your immune system, sooner or later you're bound to end up dead. And when you do (if you're a politician) you'll be libelled. This is an unavoidable fact of death. And the law is unequivocal on this important point: despite the best efforts of generations of family members and lawyers, *you can't libel the dead.*

Thus journalists, other politicians and the courts all have a time-honored tradition of blaming the dead guy. This is both effective and reasonable. After all, your old friend the dead guy doesn't care, no matter where he ended up; his family members aren't your brother politicians (or criminals, or Baptists, or judges, or whatever) so no one much cares about their feelings; and it sure as heck simplifies the paperwork. As (the late) Winston S. Churchill, a drunk, put it: "When you're dead, the little people will pee on your grave." So, in the long run, no matter how often they sue, libel is the fate of the Igor Gouzenkos of this world.

Anyway, all this assumes that you haven't been doing something *really* hinky, and they haven't got you square in their headlights.

In such circumstances, you can use a writ or even a letter from a lawyer, to delay inconvenient disclosures – "sorry, can't say anything right now, matter's before the courts" – while you pack your bags and try to get the heck out of the country. But if you've had your hand in the till and the story's likely to get the cops on your tail – or, worse, if the cops are already on their way and they've just tipped off the media to be there when they make the arrest* – you may just have to take your lumps and go to jail.

But, trust me, jail's not going to be as bad as you expected. Your kids will have a worse time on the school yard than you will in your cell. For you, it'll be clean and dry, and you'll be supported by the taxpayers – which is basically what you wanted, anyway, isn't it? So you'll be okay – as long as you're in for a nice clean financial crime, aren't all that pretty, and have no aversion to eating starchy food with plastic cutlery.

And if this is the worst that can happen, why worry? Get a novel from the prison library, make sure you grab the top bunk, and relax. . . .

---

* When it comes to being publicity hounds, the police can be unequalled, even by desperate would-be municipal politicians.

9

Dave's Handy Checklist

Some rules of engagement. A summary of essential media-manipulation techniques.

*I*n the foregoing chapters we have considered the basic techniques of media manipulation that you will require as an aspiring politician with neither an expense account nor the personal financial resources to buy hungry reporters lunch, etc. to get elected.

Should you be so fortunate as to actually win elective office, you will face the inconvenience of having to serve your constituents, or at the very least appear to. This is less true for Members of Parliament or provincial legislative assemblies, of course. But, for those of you who find yourselves at the bottom of the national political heap, it is your unfortunate duty to serve.

This is where the intermediate and advanced media-manipulation techniques we have discussed become absolutely vital. They ensure that, once elected, you will remain that way. And they insulate you effectively from annoying pressure to actually do the bidding of the voters who elected you.

This should not be viewed as an entirely selfish motive. Naturally, there is a selfish aspect to your desire to remain securely ensconced in a comfortable publicly supported position, without having to accede to the unreasonable demands of the citizenry. Nevertheless, there is an altruistic quality to your quest.

For, should people like the readers of this guidebook fail to gain and hang on to public office, their positions could be filled by citizens who actually hold the same views as most members of the taxpaying Canadian public. One does not need to be the beneficiary of a liberal college education or a subscriber to a little publicly supported magazine devoted to feminist eroticism, to realize just how bad an idea that would be!

That is precisely the kind of outcome that can make life extremely inconvenient for the people in our society who really matter, like land developers, and their spouses who serve on the boards of action committees on the status of unattractive public art or professional victimhood. Next thing you know, taxes could begin to be wasted on roads, schools and hospitals!

Thank goodness that is not about to happen. The main reason we can give thanks is effective media manipulation.

But now that you are about to embark on your political career, you will need to be able to remember a lot of stuff if you are to effectively manipulate the media. (Then again, you may just be one of those troubled souls for whom no day is complete without reading or compiling a long list of things to do.)

Luckily, I, the author of this tome, have also remembered to lay out the stuff that you most need to remember, as well as some useful additional points, in a convenient point-form format that you can photocopy and tape on your office wall or, once you are elected, on the bulletin board of your private aldermanic lounge or caucus room. Indeed, a day may come when you can even buy these points printed on stupid coffee mugs that would-be politicians' children can buy for them on the sorts of occasions that exist for greeting-card shops to sell overpriced mugs to people who can't think of anything else to get.

So, as you set out on your merry way, applying the lessons learned in previous chapters, try to bear in mind the following DOs and DON'Ts:

1) **Don't Freak Out**

So you got a bad press notice or slammed on the local radio news. So what? Answer that before you jump in front of a train, rush off to your lawyer to launch an expensive lawsuit or say something you'll soon regret. The public is fickle, and not terribly alert. Keep your trap shut and chances are all your problems will be forgotten by the close of business tomorrow.

2) **Don't Appear Desperate**

Desperation is unseemly in a grownup. It's also counterproductive. Did the pretty girls in high school go out with the most desperate guys? Of course not! Same principle applies to getting free publicity. Manipulating the news media to suit yourself should be pathetically easy. You have every reason to act with confidence.

3) **Don't Ever Pay a Public Relations Person For a Story In The Media**

Some so-called media consultants offer deals whereby you only pay if you or your product gets a favorable mention in the media. Trouble is, these guys can never resist blabbing about their scam. For reporters, who tend to be touchy about what easy marks they are anyway, the idea slices a little close. So when the word inevitably leaks, your name is mud.

4) Don't Ever Pay a Public Relations Person

Why would you? As the confident guys used to say in high school, 'Why pay for what you can get for free?' Unless, you did pay in high school or at any other time, in which case stay in the P.R. person's good graces.

5) Do Declare Your Candidacy Early and Often

More than one would-be alderman or school trustee has blown his or her chances by too much coy strategizing. Leave the striptease to the big shots. (And to the strippers, of course; but stay out of strip clubs if you want to stay elected.) You're running for town council, for heaven's sake! Announce early. Announce often.

6) Don't Answer the Question You've Just Been Asked

Never answer the question you've just been asked by a reporter! There's always a question you'd rather answer. Why not answer that one? This is especially good advice in the unlikely event the question you've just been asked is an unfriendly one.

7) Do Congratulate the Reporter on His Perspicacious Query Before Answering Another Question You'd Rather Answer

Of course you're not going to answer the question you've just been asked. But that shouldn't stop you from saying something like, "That's a very good question, Bob. . . ." before answering the question that suits you better.

8) Do Blame Someone Else

If flattery has gotten you nowhere, and you're still cornered, blame someone else. Blame the mayor, blame the U.S. economy, blame the Bundesbank, blame Australian canola farmers, blame whoever. But, in this game, never, ever take responsibility for anything bad.

9) Do Walk Away From Hard Questions

Feeling mugged by the media after a tough council meeting? Plead a rush call to the private aldermanic washroom and exit by the back door. Had a pleasant media scrum suddenly turn nasty? Have a flunky announce you've got a plane to catch and march briskly away. Always leave with a smile on your face and a confident wave of the hand.

10) Do Only Hear Questions That Suit You

You've been mobbed by reporters, the usual embarrassing questions about your pending bankruptcy are being asked by the usual suspects. But the spear-carrier from the local country radio station asks you about your free-parking initiative. Guess which question you ought to answer.

11) Do Always Have a Pet Reporter

If you don't have a favorite reporter, who's going to ask you friendly questions in unfriendly situations? (For tips on how to get and keep a pet reporter, see Chapter 7.) However, *don't* take this to mean you can't phone up another reporter if your pet's not in the mood.

12) Do String Out a Friendly Question

If you just can't escape a mob scene where ugly sentiments are being expressed by the press, don't hesitate to string out your response to a friendly question asked by a pet. With any luck, the bell summoning councillors to the voting chamber will begin clanging before you're done. Smile apologetically – and dash!

13) Don't Repeat Negative Questions

Never, never, never do this. In public life, there's always a recording device spinning somewhere nearby. If you feel you absolutely must answer a negative question, rephrase it in a much more self-serving manner. Better, however, to simply answer another question entirely.

14) Do Speak into the Mike in 30-second Clips

At least, in friendly one-on-one interviews with confused radio and television reporters, which pretty well describes them all, try to frame your answers in hard-to-edit bursts about half a minute long. But don't use this technique when under assault by an unfriendly mob of reporters. In such circumstances, see hint No.12 above.

15) Do Throw Everyone a Bone Now and Then

Even to reporters you hate. Otherwise they'll just hate you more and, more important, will only talk to sources who hate you. At business luncheons, throwing everyone a bone like this is called being "pro-active." I've often said, "I'm going to throttle the next moron who says 'pro-active.'" I haven't done it yet, though.

16) Do Shower 'em with Paper

Idle hands are the Devil's workshop. Many reporters may be too lazy to ease their duffs off the divan for anything but a free jelly donut, but why take the chance? Keep 'em busy with a steady stream of news releases, all written up so that they can be signed and filed as the reporter's "own" copy as painlessly and swiftly as possible.

17) Do Leak Confidential Documents

While we're talking steady streams, nothing so successfully cements a relationship between a politician and a pet reporter as a steady stream of leaked documents. The only people you're going to offend are senior bureaucrats. They have their own agendas, which are not the same as yours. If you don't believe this, don't give up your day job. You'd be back at it soon enough anyway.

18) Don't Always Insist on Buying Lunch

But *do* always offer. (This obviously doesn't apply if you don't have an expense account yet.) Some reporters retain remnants of dignity. Such people will be embarrassed if you push them to take your hospitality too soon. Don't put them in a difficult position – they'll come meekly to you in time.

19) Do Threaten One Reporter with Another

News reporters are competitive If you give one a dumb story idea that serves your interests, he may just drop it. Tell him the woman from the competition has it, and vice versa, and they'll both probably do what you want to avoid being scooped.

20) Don't Ever Tell Jokes About Women or Minorities, Even if They're *Really* Funny

If you haven't figured this one out, you belong in some other line of work — like maybe journalism. Remember that tape recorder? It's always running.

21) Don't Lie Outright

You may trip up. Why take the risk when you can always answer another question?

22) Don't Put Your Faith in God in Writing

This is Canada, not Rome or Salt Lake City. In a speech, maybe. On a doorstep, sure. But never mention your faith, no matter how sincere, in a news release. Put it in a handout, and the godless media will dismiss you as a loony-tune. Either that, or they'll mistake it for a reference to a 12-step group's higher power and conclude you're a substance abuser. Count on it, either way, you'll lose the election.*

23) Do Be Available For Quotes at Any Hour, Any Place

Easy girls get all the action. Ditto for easy quotes. If you develop some sort of bogus expertise on something or other — council's finance guru, say — so much the better.

24) Don't Whine

Nothing's more irritating than a politician who's constantly reminding reporters about how his great accomplishments have been unjustly ignored by the press. It may be true, but who cares? Stop snivelling and start leaking documents!

---

* Here's a verifiable quote from an actual candidate's news release, circa 1993: "Each and every year of my life, I see more clearly just how relevant our Bible and its parables are to our modern life today. . . ." Needless to say, the author's political dreams fell on stony ground.

25) Do Patronize Broadcast Reporters On the Air

But only a little. Your viewers and supporters expect reporters to address you as Mr. or Ms. or even Doctor; it's a Canadian custom. And they expect you to address them back as Bob, Vickie and the like. This is of course mildly insulting, so try to make it up to them when the tapes are turned off by offering lunch, pretending to listen to their advice, or getting one of your flunkies to press their shirts.

26) Do Keep Trying

There's always another reporter, a slow news day is coming. Keep phoning, dropping off news releases, announcing your intentions. Sooner or later, out of boredom, inattention or sheer stupefaction, someone will reprint or rebroadcast your self-serving bumf. Just keep in mind: successfully manipulating the media is usually easy to do.

27) Don't Threaten to Sue

By all means sue for defamation, but don't utter baseless threats. That's what you pay your lawyer to do. If you do plan to sue, of course, it's always best to select someone relatively defenceless, like a student newspaper or community newsletter, over a big organization with its own legal department.

28) Don't Threaten, Period

Same as for lawsuits, never threaten journalists with physical violence. Same reasons. There's nothing like a threat of violence to tip off a reporter that he's dealing with a really pathetic, powerless geek. If you simply must resort to mayhem, let your fists make the announcement.

29) Don't Fall for the Here's-What-I'm-Gonna-Write Gambit

When a reporter tries this one with an unfriendly story, he's trying to goad you into saying something stupid. Instead, chuckle and say, "Just go ahead and print that and see what happens. . . . Heh-heh-heh."

30) Don't Mention Your Political Foes

Why give them the air or the ink? If you must respond to something, don't refer to them by name. "Well, only a homo sapiens and a bibliophile would say that. . . ."

31) Don't Go Off the Record

Oh heck, go ahead and go off the record. Makes reporters feel like big shots. Just make sure you don't gossip about something that'll make you sound like a fool when it leaks out that you said it, as it invariably will. In other words, don't say anything off the record that you wouldn't say on the record.

32) Do Be Available

If you're nobody and see being quoted a lot as a key to becoming somebody, you must be available night and day. If you're called at 3 a.m. by a reporter asking if you're against things that might kill your constituents, answer politely and at length. Act as if you take him seriously. After all, if he's calling at that hour, no one else will talk to him and you're likely to get good play.

33) Do Be Quick

Remember, many reporters are almost breathtakingly lazy. If one calls during the daylight hours and you get back quickly with a pithy quote or two, chances are he won't bother to call anyone else and you'll have the whole story to yourself and your harebrained notions. This is called "setting the agenda."

34) Do Be First

Or biggest, or fastest, or loudest. The media loves superlatives. The first baby of the new year is big news. The second? Pfft! So if you're not first, or whatever, declare yourself so in a news release, "[put your name here] will be the youngest alderman ever elected in our fair city. . . ." Someone will bite.

35) Don't Remind Them

Yes, the media loves "firsts," but the rule gets reversed in the face of real catastrophes. One weenie gets amputated by a spouse and news editors all over the world are on the lookout for other similar missing members. A village councillor in New Brunswick gets busted for drunk driving and the next thing you know your two-year-old conviction's back in the news.*

36) Don't Ask to See a Story Before It's Published

At least, don't ask until you've established an enduring and satisfying relationship with your pet reporter. If you ask too soon, you'll get nowhere. Just be patient and buy a couple more lunches.

37) Do Remember the Media Can Dish It Out But They Can't Take It

If you crossed a wild boar with most reporters, you'd get a pig that can hold a grudge. So if you foolishly respond sharply to something that makes you deeply unhappy, prepare to face years of whining, lawsuits and threats of human rights investigations. Why bother when successful manipulation is easier? So. . . .

38) Don't Freak Out

Did we say this? Yeah, well, it never hurts to repeat the obvious. When you're about to freak out, just remember the words of a great Canadian copy editor, gone now for the great fishinghole in the sky: "Only about a quarter of the people in this town read this crummy paper, and only about a quarter of them read that story, and only about a quarter of them believed it, and only about a quarter of them cared, and that's just two guys, and they're of no damn account anyway!"

So, you now know pretty well all you need to know to successfully manipulate the media with the objective of launching your political career, or, at the very least, not humiliating yourself and losing your $100 deposit.

Above all, some reporters have figured this all out – including, for example, those of my colleagues who have bought this book and studied its contents. This list should help you avoid most of

---

* This gives rise to the Bus Plunge Syndrome. Buses full of passengers that plunge over precipices have become an enduring in-group joke in journalism. The term "bus plunge" describes a story describing a bus plunge. As in, "I've got a hole on the bottom of page 97 that'll take that bus plunge." When you see the phrase in a headline – "Forty die in bus plunge" – a small joke is being had at your expense.

the pitfalls that await those embarking on a political career. But, with luck, my fellow journalists will keep coming up with enough new material to justify a sequel to this book.

Until then, good luck and bon voyage!

Graduate Studies

Appendix Introduction

Those would-be politicians and others who are going to have to do their own typing – which will describe many of the readers of this book – it is often helpful to have some words at your fingertips. Likewise, some book-buyers are just so anally retentive (does that take a hyphen?) that they have to know *all* the details to feel they've gotten their money's worth. The two following appendices are for such readers.

They comprise two actual news releases – one quite effective, the other not – for which professional public relations people were actually paid perfectly good taxpayers' money. Accompanying them is some commentary by the author about what has been done right, and what has not.

Appendix I

An actual news release, with minimal changes to disguise the identities of the innocent, et al.

LIBRARY BOARD INTRODUCES CHANGES TO BALANCE BUDGET

With the aim of balancing a shrinking operating budget, the _____ Public Library Board today announced a number of changes to fees, hours and services which will go into effect January 1, 1994.

Library Director Leon Blotz explained that the decision to introduce these changes was made in anticipation of funding cuts from both the City and the Province.

"Reduced operating grants are becoming reality in today's economy. We wanted to be ready for them by making adjustments which would have minimal impact on our customers," said Blotz. "All the changes we are introducing are based on the results of surveys conducted over the past two years which indicated customers would opt for some service cuts and fee increases rather than face a tax hike."

In the new year, the registration processing/annual renewal fee for adults' and seniors' library cards will go up by $1; adults' cards will now be $6 and seniors' cards will be $3. Young adults' cards (for 13- to 17-year-olds) will remain at $2, and cards for children 12 and under will still be free.

Seniors will no longer be exempt from paying fines for overdue materials. A new $2 fine will also be applied to the account of any customer who places a library item on hold and then neglects to pick up the item.

As a result of extensive research on peak times of library usage, hours will be altered at a number of library locations. The _____ Central Library will open at 10 a.m. instead of 9 a.m., Monday to Saturday. To increase consistency and efficiency, hours at neighbourhood and community branches will be standardized and reduced slightly.

Due to a heavy volume of telephone inquiries and limited staff resources, customers will now be asked to visit their local branch to obtain information about the titles and due dates of materials borrowed. This will allow customers to see their own borrowing records on the computer screen and avoid waiting on the telephone for long periods.

Rates for renting the _____ Theatre or library meeting rooms will increase moderately in 1994 while remaining competitive, and room rentals will be limited to six library locations.

Due to high repair/maintenance costs, the availability of commercial rental services, and the relatively low customer demand, our projector rental service will be discontinued.

"We are the busiest . . . public facility in _____. It is simply impossible to absorb funding cuts from two levels of government without making some changes to the service and fee structure," said Blotz. "So far, we have been able to make changes that will create a minimum of inconvenience for our customers. Unfortunately, additional cutbacks may be necessary as funding constraint continues at both the municipal and provincial levels of government.

"That being the case, we need to work more closely than ever with our customers to minimize the impact of those changes. _____ will have to realize that small actions – for example, remembering to renew library cards – make a tremendous difference to the viability of our operations."

_____ Public Library has introduced several initiatives in the past year to improve efficiency and increase revenues, including a three-year strategic plan and a card marketing and awareness campaign. Plans are also under way to launch a fund-raising campaign in 1994.

-30-

For more information, contact:
Leon Blotz, Director
OR
Marcia Maplethorpe, Manager, Communications.

Dave's note: Really, aside from being a trifle over-long, this news release is nearly perfect. For something entirely different, compare it with the release in Appendix II.

APPENDIX II

About Public Relations and an actual ineffective news release.

A Note on Public Relations

The curse of being a staff public relations functionary, and the reason no sane person would knowingly choose flackery of this sort as a career or even a pastime, is that nobody will ever believe anything you say.

Your employers will never tell you anything, viewing you as a kind of in-house reporter, not to be trusted. You will be expected, however, to immediately ensure that no one is ever bothered by reporters and that the media is crammed with favorable stories about your employer. The media, in turn, will revile you as a paid liar and, since they will soon recognize you know absolutely nothing about what's going on, will ignore you and go straight to your boss. The resulting fracas will enrage both. So, in not very much time, both groups will grow to hate you because you simply cannot do your job.

This is especially true in government. There, as likely as not, the PR functionary's ultimate political boss is the kind of illiterate glad-hander so often elected in small-town Canada, the kind of fellow who figures that since he made it selling General Motors cars in the days when GM cars still more or less worked and GM had the only dealership network around anyway, that he doesn't need advice from anybody on anything – especially, matters pertaining to politics. After all, he reasons (with some justice) he got elected, didn't he? Which is more than most of these college graduates could do!

Worse, the suffering flack's direct supervisor is almost certainly the kind of toadying political crony that can so often be found buzzing profitably around the more questionable fringes of public service.

As a result, regardless of how good a PR flack's advice is, it is virtually certain never to be taken, or even listened to.

This is ironic, because – when it comes to government PR people, at any rate – their advice tends to be pretty sound. This is because, typically, thanks to the scrupulous fairness of most Canadian public service commissions, almost anyone on a public payroll who is not a political appointee is good at their job, or at least properly qualified to do it. (This flies in the face of the self-serving mythology of the private sector, of course.) Second, because people who refuse to listen to the good advice from their staff flacks often end up listening and doing the most imbecilic things imaginable when advised by a highly paid consultant – a member of a class populated almost entirely by nincompoop charlatans. (People pay a lot for bad advice because paying a lot makes them feel like big shots; they take the bad advice because, well, they've paid a lot for it. This makes them double bone-heads.)

This peculiar mix of circumstances gives rise to a curious phenomenon: thoroughly competent public-sector PR flacks that draft, over their own pleas and objections, bizarre and incomprehensible media handouts on the orders of their brain-dead private-sector-trained superiors.

We will call this peculiar type of statement, for the lack of a more humorous appellation, the public-service news release. It arises from the pathetic need of many politicians to see their names in print without having to develop eye-strain from reading down more than one or two sentences, and to quickly establish a pecking order among their colleagues in public life.

The conventions of the form are long lists of names and titles in the initial paragraphs, a nearly total absence of information usable by journalists, heavy reliance on incomprehensible jargon, and ham-handed attempts to steer readers away from matters not properly explained. The initial lists of titles become particularly hilarious when various levels of government or different agencies must get together to try to announce a joint program. You can almost hear the various ministers and directors cursing each other as they jostle and elbow for position.

The unintended and often comic result of a public service news release is the complete opposite of what any competent news release strives to achieve. Instead of providing a tempting-to-reprint faux news story with an upbeat spin – like the release in the previous appendix – the statement practically begs even the most incompetent or uncaring journalistic hack to do his worst. The catalog of names and titles demands stinging shots or, even better, no reference whatsoever to the luminaries listed therein. The impenetrable jargon and dangling references to unexplained controversies simply dare reporters to call up and ask difficult questions about such obviously dishonest evasions, or better yet to canvass groups of likely critics and opponents for stinging rebuttals. And since the listed contacts are almost never where they are supposed to be, the net effect is to turn the reporter's extreme irritation on reading this kind of stuff into outright near-homicidal rage.

Consider the following actual news release (I'm not making up this) – a nearly perfect example of the class. It fails delightfully on almost every line, at every level. It begins with a bogus embargo – something ignored by all sensible news operations on the reasonable ground that, if something's been printed and mailed, it's been published – and it ends with three contact people, not one of whom was anywhere near a telephone the afternoon your correspondent had the misfortune to have to try to deal with it.

In between, it has attention-grabbing holes big enough to accommodate a Peterbilt 18-wheeler, it fails to disguise the obviously evasive intent of the government to put off making a decision about whatever the release was about, and it is thick with the laughably contrived-sounding quotes and ridiculous jargon beloved of the terminally self-important. It has so many misplaced punctuation marks and capital letters, and is so little like a real news story, that it simply begs for aggressive editing – a sin in any quasi-journalistic composition, even one of mine. And it even commences with a reminder that it's old news! In short, it does virtually everything wrong that a press release can do wrong.

I have no knowledge of the circumstances that led to the drafting of this handout. I can only assure readers that it is simply not credible that it was willingly composed by a competent government public relations flack. No, this one smacks of political interference of the worst sort at the highest levels, and it deserves whatever fate it received. (Any country newspaper editor who ran it verbatim, and there are sure to have been a couple, deserves a sound horsewhipping.)

So here it is, the thoroughly hilarious composition, generously sprinkled capital letters, missing commas, extra commas, and all. Only a few changes were made to avoid embarrassing the guilty needlessly. I warn you, there is nothing charming about what you are about to read:

GOVERNMENT OF FAR PETROLIA

For immediate release: February 9, 1994

EMBARGO: 9:00 a.m.

GREAT PLACES 3000 REPORT RELEASED FOR PUBLIC REVIEW

Oilpan City – Barney Rubblski, Deputy Premier and Minister of Economic Development and Tourism and Calvin Garfield, Minister of Environmental Protection today released for public review, the report of the Great Places 3000 Advisory Committee. Committee Chairman, Bleak-Hollow-Moose-Knuckle MLA Ernie Greystoke, first presented the report to the ministers for their review in mid-November of 1993.

"Great Places 3000 is a component of 'Seizing Opportunity,' our new economic development and social strategy," said Mr. Rubblski. "Today's report brings us closer to completing that component. I would like to thank the committee for their efforts and their thoughts on what may be included in a Policy Statement on Great Places 3000. As well, I want to recognize my late cabinet colleague Dagwood Bumstead for originating this important initiative."

"This report is an important milestone in the Great Places 3000 initiative," said Mr. Garfield. "Its recommendations are the result of our discussions with Far Petrolians, and reflect our Premier's commitment to open government and public consultation. I would also like to commend Ernie Greystoke and his committee for their hard work in consulting with Far Petrolians and preparing this report. I am looking forward to discussing it further with my caucus colleagues and to endorsing a policy and developing a plan to implement a system of Great Places by the year 3000."

The report and public reaction to its contents will be used as input to finalize government policy on the Great Places initiative. A 60 day period to examine the report and provide comments on its recommendations will be provided. Concurrent with the public review, Mr. Garfield noted that his colleagues will be reviewing the report and providing their thoughts on it. Upon completion of the review period the ministers will bring the proposed policy, along with public and interdepartmental comments, to the Standing Policy Committee on Natural resources and Sustainable Development and then to cabinet for review and approval. Cabinet is expected to release a response to the report shortly thereafter.

"The Great Places 3000 Advisory report, in particular the recommendations on the site selection process, will need to be assessed to determine its support of the economic and environmental values set out in 'Seizing Opportunity'," said Mr. Rubblski. "The period provided for public input will help the government develop a final policy on Great Places 3000."

Committee chairman Ernie Greystoke said, "this report presents the views of many Far Petrolians from all sectors; public, private and corporate. I believe its recommendations will form the foundation for a comprehensive policy and action plan for completing a Great Places network in Far Petrolia."

The public is requested to provide written comments on the report to the offices of the Minister of Environmental Protection, 42 Legislature Building or the Minister of Economic Development and Tourism, 696 Legislature Building Oilpan City.*

- 30 -

Contact:

Adain Bumby – Environmental Protection

Rex "Blondie" Morgan – Economic Development and Tourism

Ernie Greystoke – MLA Bleak-Hollow-Moose-Knuckle

---

* Possible translation: "We spent a load on this sucker and we'd better say something, but there's no agreement in cabinet about opening new parks when we're talking about privatizing old ones. Let's stall for two months and see if the tree-huggers bug off or the Premier fires one of the big players."

Glossary of Media Terms

Some of these terms even appear in the text. All of them will help you sound like you know what you're talking about as you try to cement your first relationship with a pet journalist or impress the hell out of your new colleagues on council or the school board.

ALDERMAN: Pretty much as low as you can get in politics in Canada and still get paid.

ANGLE: A new way of approaching an old story in the forlorn hope of turning a sow's ear into a silk purse. As in, "What's the angle on this story?"

ART: A newspaper and magazine term for photos and illustrations. Also the friendly guy on the loading dock.

BACKGROUND: Also deep background. See OFF THE RECORD.

BIMBO: Once a female television reporter; now any male reporter nowadays – alternately HIMBO.

BN: Broadcast News. The radiophonic equivalent of a WIRE SERVICE.

BYLINE: The line of type that says who wrote a newspaper story. It is the only known measure of journalistic productivity, despite claims to the contrary. Tells would-be media manipulators who to stroke or threaten.

CAMERA PERSON: The source of most of the intelligent questions asked by television journalists.

COMMUNITY ACTIVIST: A busybody incapable of getting elected community association president, let alone alderman or school trustee.

CONFIDENTIAL: Just about anything done or said by a Canadian public employee.

COPY EDITOR: The guy who writes the headlines. Reporters *never* write headlines. So yelling at your reporter about a headline gets you worse than nowhere.

CNN: Where most newspapers get their information.

CRIME NEWS: A golden opportunity for RENT-A-MOUTHs to provide REACTION.

DEADLINE: The last moment at which a news story may be submitted for publication or broadcast. As deadlines approach, reporters grow more desperate, hence more likely to use quotes from COMMUNITY ACTIVISTS.

DEFAMATION: A libel or slander. Defamatory words written or spoken that can't be proven in a court of law to be true and fair, even if they are. Suing for defamation is an effective way to suppress criticism or get revenge on uncooperative reporters.

DESKER: A newspaper copy editor. Copy editors sit on "the desk," or (worse) "around the rim" (don't ask, it's not as bad as it sounds), deskers are the hard core of competence on any daily newspaper.

EXECUTIVE ASSISTANT: A formal title for a fart-catcher.

EXISTENTIAL LEAD: A way of beginning a news story in the present tense – "Jesus is weeping" – that almost invariably signals a boring and pointless waste of time.

FART-CATCHER: A political or business aide, so named for obvious reasons.

FLACK: Also FLAK. Commonly used term for a public relations huckster. Once pejorative, increasingly less so. Flacks are the principal supporters of North America's few surviving "press clubs."

FREE LUNCH: Some economists will tell you there is no such thing; many generous politicians prove them wrong daily.

HACK: Any journalistic writer. Also HACKETTES, and SPAVINED HACKS.

HUMAN INTEREST STORY: A feature news story on the air or in print for which no other conceivable justification exists; human interest stories are often not even about humans and only rarely interesting.

HYPE: Torquing up a news story so that it seems more significant than it really is. For example, if the words job cuts are first in a hyped story, the words attrition and no actual layoffs won't put in an appearance until quite a bit later.

INITIATIVE: Anything a politician does or doesn't do.

INVERSE PYRAMID: See WIRE-SERVICE STYLE.

LAPTOP COMMUTER: A public transportation user who wastes time on tabloid newspapers.

LEAK: Any unauthorized release of confidential information.

LIBEL: A defamation in any permanent form, including video tape. Virtually the only libels that ever see court action, however, are those in print. Broadcasters can usually say pretty much what they feel like and get away with it because nobody's really paying attention.

LOCALIZER: A feeble attempt to make a news staff look more capable than it really is by handing a reporter a national story and telling him to find "the local angle" and stick it on the top.

MEDIA: Unless you're a pedant, it's not a plural noun; a gathering of fortunetellers.

MEDIA EVENT: About halfway between a photo opportunity and a news conference.

MEDIA KIT: A news release packaged with a business card, a sheet of "background" information and a couple of photographs in a cute cardboard folder. Not likely to impress anyone, and seldom worth the expense.

MUG SHOT: A head-and-shoulders photo used to illustrate a news story. After (and sometimes preceding) the police photograph of the same name.

NEWSER: Journalistic shorthand for a news conference, which is in turn a contrived media event designed to manipulate reporters into feeling important and writing favorable reports about whatever bogus "initiative" is being announced.

NEWS RELEASE: A self-serving publicity handout designed to pass for an actual news story. Too much of what you read in the paper and see on TV is a news release once removed. Also known as a press release.

OFF THE RECORD: Gossip you don't want your name associated with, much of it malicious.

PHOTO OPPORTUNITY: A newser without the opportunity to ask even softball questions. No work and lots of sticky buns! Good for everyone but the public.

PLAY: Where in the newscast or newspaper a story appears.

PRESS CLUB: The sort of place flacks used to go to buy drinks for hacks, thus preserving an illusion of influence. Their clients, and the clubs themselves, are now withering away as health-obsessed boomer journalists forsake the bar for the barbells.

PUFFERY: What flacks always write; what too many Canadian journalists are expected to write. Not to be confused with Puffy, Mike, a television personality.

REACTION: In modern journalism, for every action, no matter how idiotic, there must be an equal and opposite reaction. Hence, an opportunity for politicians to see their names in print.

RENT-A-MOUTH: Someone who can be depended upon to deliver a quotable quote on anything, anywhere, anytime.

SCHOOL TRUSTEE: Lower than an alderman, but still paid.

SCOOP: An exclusive news story. Scoops are generally frowned upon in an era when a lot of journalists prefer to follow the herd and not be responsible for pursuing a story not done first elsewhere.

SCRUM: An unruly mob of reporters desperately clamoring for senseless quotes.

SLANDER: A sensible Common Law tort dealing with spoken defamation. Canadian defamation law, naturally, leans heavily on the Star Chamber tort of libel, which gives all the advantages to the litigious politician.

SPIN: A self-serving interpretation of events.

SPIN-DOCTOR: A fart-catcher who makes a living buying journalists lunch and interpreting events in ways that make his boss look good.

STREETER: Journalistic argot for a man-in-the-street interview, best described as the unintelligent in pursuit of the unintelligible.

TAKE: Something politicians do with decisions. The rest of us make 'em. Sort of like tax dollars, come to think of it.

TORQUE: When used by a journalist, hype; when used by a pollster, spin. Not to be confused with *toque*, a kind of hat.

THIRTY: The accepted way to end a press release, because it was once the customary way to end the first draft of a news story, traditionally written - 30 - .

VILLAGE COUNCILLOR: Lower than a school trustee, which is a toss up with reeve.

WIRE SERVICE: An organization that absolves local newspapers of the expense of having to employ their own poorly paid hacks.

WIRE-SERVICE STYLE: An uninformative and difficult-to-follow way of writing that makes it easy for newspapers to cram any story into any corner, hence saving money at the expense of clarity.

WIRE-SERVICE SPORTS WRITER: A group of people who describe themselves as the lowest form of animal life.